RURA
THE UNTAPPED
POTENTIAL

Dr. Abhishek Mukherjee

INDIA • SINGAPORE • MALAYSIA

Notion Press Media Pvt Ltd

No. 50, Chettiyar Agaram Main Road,
Vanagaram, Chennai, Tamil Nadu – 600 095

First Published by Notion Press 2021
Copyright © Dr. Abhishek Mukherjee 2021
All Rights Reserved.

ISBN 978-1-63904-647-8

This book has been published with all efforts taken to make the material error-free after the consent of the author. However, the author and the publisher do not assume and hereby disclaim any liability to any party for any loss, damage, or disruption caused by errors or omissions, whether such errors or omissions result from negligence, accident, or any other cause.

While every effort has been made to avoid any mistake or omission, this publication is being sold on the condition and understanding that neither the author nor the publishers or printers would be liable in any manner to any person by reason of any mistake or omission in this publication or for any action taken or omitted to be taken or advice rendered or accepted on the basis of this work. For any defect in printing or binding the publishers will be liable only to replace the defective copy by another copy of this work then available.

Dedication

This book is dedicated to all the aspirants who want to become entrepreneurs and start their own venture by tapping the Rural Women Potential which still remains untapped.

Contents

Foreword — 11
Preface — 13
About the Book — 17
Acknowledgements — 21
About the Author — 23

Chapter 1 Self-Analysis — 25
    Learning Objectives: — 25
    Learning Outcome: — 25
    Chapter Outline: — 26
    Self-Analysis: — 26
        1.1 Introduction: — 26
        1.2 Self-Analysis: — 28
        1.3 Need for Self Analysis: — 29
        1.4 Importance of Self Analysis: — 31
        1.5 How to do Self-Analysis? — 32
        Summary: — 33

Chapter 2 Skill Analysis — 34

Learning Objectives: — 34

Learning Outcomes: — 34

Chapter Outline: — 35

2. Skills Analysis: — 35

    2.1 Introduction: — 35

    2.2 What is a Skill? — 36

    2.3 Types of Skills: — 37

    2.4 What is Skill Analysis? — 38

    2.5 Need and Importance of Skill Analysis: — 39

    2.6 How to analyze one's own skills? — 40

    2.7 How to convert your Skills into a Vocation? — 41

    Summary: — 44

Chapter 3 Employment Vs Self-Employment — 45

Learning Objectives: — 45

Learning Outcomes: — 46

Chapter Outline: — 46

3. Employment Vs Self Employment: — 46

    3.1 Introduction: — 46

    3.2 Employment – Meaning and Definition: — 47

    3.3 What is a Job? — 47

    3.4 Self-Employment: — 48

    3.5 Forms of Self Employment: — 48

    3.6 Need for Self-Employment: — 49

    3.7 Importance of Self-Employment: — 49

    3.8 Comparative Analysis of Job and Self-Employment — 53

    Summary: — 54

Chapter 4 Entrepreneurial Mindset	56
Learning Objectives:	56
Learning Outcomes:	57
Chapter Outline:	57
4. Entrepreneurial Mindset:	57
4.1 Introduction:	57
4.2 What is Entrepreneurial Mindset?	58
4.3 How Entrepreneurial Mindset is different?	58
4.4 Characteristics of Entrepreneurial Mindset:	59
4.5 Factors Leading to Entrepreneurial Mindset:	60
4.6 Creativity and Innovation:	62
4.7 Positive results of Entrepreneurial Mindset:	62
Summary:	64
Chapter 5 Self-Employment Avenues	66
Learning Objectives:	66
Learning Outcomes:	67
Chapter Outline:	67
5. Self-Employment Avenues:	67
5.1 Introduction:	67
5.2 Self-Employment Avenues Identified for Rural Women:	68
5.3 Self-Employment Avenues Identified for Women in Urban Areas:	73
5.5 How to Avail the Avenues of Self-Employment and Entrepreneurship:	73
5.6 Factors Influencing Rural Women towards Entrepreneurship:	74
5.7 Challenges faced by Rural Women Entrepreneurs:	77
Summary:	80

Chapter 6 Entrepreneurial Environment — 82

- Learning Objectives: — 82
- Learning Outcomes: — 83
- Chapter Outline: — 83
- 6. Entrepreneurial Environment: — 83
  - 6.1 Introduction: — 83
  - 6.2 What is Entrepreneurial Environment? — 84
  - 6.3 Need for Entrepreneurial Environment: — 84
  - 6.4 Importance of Entrepreneurial Environment: — 85
  - 6.5 Creation of Entrepreneurial Environment: — 86
  - 6.6 Support System of Entrepreneurial Environment: — 89
- Summary: — 90

Chapter 7 Hand Holding — 91

- Learning Objectives: — 91
- Learning Outcomes: — 91
- Chapter Outline: — 92
- 7. Hand Holding: — 92
  - 7.1 Introduction: — 92
  - 7.2 What is Hand Holding? — 93
  - 7.3 Need and Importance of Hand Holding: — 93
  - 7.4 How Hand Holding can be done? — 94
  - 7.5 Benefits of Hand Holding: — 96
- Summary: — 98

Chapter 8 Training Requirements and Avenues — 100

- Learning Objectives: — 100
- Learning Outcomes: — 100
- Chapter Outline: — 101

8.	Training Requirement Avenues:	101
	8.1 Introduction:	101
	8.2 Identification of Training Needs:	102
	8.3 Areas in which Practical Training is Required:	103
	8.4 Institutes Imparting Training to Rural Women:	104
	8.5 Short Term Courses for Rural Women:	105
	Summary:	110

Chapter 9 How to Raise Funds? — 111

Learning Objectives: — 111
Learning Outcomes: — 111
Chapter Outline: — 112

9. How to Raise Funds? — 112
    - 9.1 Introduction: — 112
    - 9.2 Identification of Funds Requirement: — 114
    - 9.3 Areas where Funds will be required: — 114
    - 9.4 Sources to Raise Funds: — 119
    - Summary: — 123

Chapter 10 Establishing your Own Start-Up — 124

Learning Objectives: — 124
Learning Outcome: — 124
Chapter Outline: — 125

10. Establishing your own Start-Up: — 125
    - 10.1 Introduction: — 125
    - 10.2 What is a Start-Up? — 126
    - 10.3 Need and Importance of Start-Up: — 127
    - 10.4 Step by Step Procedure to Establish One's Own Start-Up: — 129
    - Summary: — 134

Foreword

Woman – The word is still a mystery for many. For ages women have been considered and made to be dormant, waking up only to cater to the needs of the men and their family, to bring new lives in to the world and give them a good upbringing. Todays' woman, though still a mystery for some, has come out of her nutshell and has learned to move ahead with time. We can see many women who are excellent homemakers, who along with nurturing a family also make their children self-reliant and confident.

Today women are present in all walks of life and are succeeding in all their roles. Men have also changed over the years, realizing the potential of women, giving them equal importance and position in their lives and supporting them in their endeavors. But this is more present in urban areas. What about the rural areas? Just because a woman lives in rural area it does not mean that she is dumb or incapable. She is just like a bomb waiting to explode. She just needs the correct ignition at the right time to get started and no one can stop her from exploding. What is needed is to instill the confidence and know-how in her and she will succeed with flying colours.

This book "Rural Women – The Untapped potential" has showcased the unexplored potential which is present in the rural women. This book has come at the right time when our country is moving forward towards being 'Atma Nirbhar' i.e. Self-Reliant. The book throws light on the employment prospects available in the rural areas which will prove to be a boon to us and our country when they are utilized properly.

It takes a different mind set to become an entrepreneur. Being an entrepreneur requires certain set of skills. Though many would like to become an entrepreneur, the lack of knowledge about how to begin and go about the same makes it difficult for many and they end up being a job taker instead of a job giver. This book is a complete guide for those who are willing to become an entrepreneur. It talks about the entrepreneurial mindset, the skills required and how to analyze your skills, the training requirements for the same, how to analyze oneself, the legal procedures involved in establishing a startup and how to raise funds for the same etc.

First and foremost, what is important is the willingness to take a plunge in the deep sea of entrepreneurship. This willingness to pen a book on his experience is what has made Dr. Abhishek Mukherjee an author today. This book will act as a guide to all those who have the guts and the mindset to do something of their own. My heartfelt congratulations to Dr. Abhishek Mukherjee on his first book which I am sure will change many lives and help many achieve their dream of becoming an entrepreneur.

Dr. Devendra Bhave

Associate Professor & Vice Principal

Sanskar Mandir's Arts and Commerce College, Warje-Malwadi,

Pune.

Preface

This book "Rural Women – The Untapped Potential" exhumes the potential which is hidden in 'Rural Women' which I found while doing my research in the rural areas of Pune while visiting 13 talukas of Pune Rural. During my research journey I found that only having potential is not enough. You are a Diamond but the value of 'Diamond' can be only understood by a lapidarist. Monkey does not understand the value of Diamond. If a monkey is given a diamond, he will just throw it away as he feels it is a stone. In the same manner the Rural Women have huge potential but require people to unleash their potential. Because of lack of literacy, awareness, exposure and education their potential remains untapped. This book is an effort to exhume the potential hidden in Rural Women and how can Rural Women be made "Atma Nirbhar".

The first and the foremost thing which is important is that you need to say it to your own Self that 'I Can Do This'. Self-confidence is very important but at the same time there should be people around you who will make you feel confident. Sometimes we come across negative people and negative environment who try to demotivate and restrict us from achieving our goals. "A Failure Person Can Never Teach You Lessons of Success." A successful person can only give you the Mantras of how to become one. Self-Analysis is very important. The maximum amount of time a person stays with someone is One Own Self. Hence the Best Person who knows your capabilities are you – yourself. Don't follow Rat Race. You are unique on this earth. Try to preserve your uniqueness. Don't do things which others are doing. Do what you are capable at. It is often seen that people do things following others. They don't understand the utility of doing a particular thing. I am choosing Science because my friends are choosing that Subject. I want to become doctor because my friend has also opted for the same profession. When I was in 10th standard, it was a preconceived notion that either you will have to take Science i.e. Physics, Chemistry and Mathematics and become an Engineer or else take Science with Physics, Chemistry, Botany and Zoology and become a Doctor. If you are not able to choose either of the Subjects, then 'You are a Duffer' and your future is in dark. But the reality is something different. There is plethora of career opportunities where in people can join and achieve success and mint money. The only thing which is required is an introspection.

Sometimes even after doing Self-Analysis we are unable to figure out What am I good at? In that case, it becomes quite evident that someone should tell me that – Hey You. Yes, you. You have these skills. Please pursue those skills and develop on them. Hence Skill Analysis is equally important. We all need a mentor or a guide who will test my skills and give me a proper direction as to which path to follow. Every vocation, requires a particular skill. Not all five fingers are same. In the same way don't compare yourself with others.

The next decision which you need to take is whether you want to take up a job or give jobs. "Maalik Banna Hai Ya Naukar". The problem with the current education system is that everybody wants to do a Job. Even after pursuing a 'Business Administration' and 'Business Management Program', students are not learning how to do Business. Doing Business is a Skill and hence is not everyone's cup of tea. Self-Employment is the need of the hour. But then all the Questions arise? What? When? Who? Where? How? Whom?

For becoming an entrepreneur and starting your own start-up and undergoing self-employment requires a lot of courage. Because there is always a lot of discouragement from family, friends, colleagues and society as well. This is because starting your business requires entrepreneurial mindset. The entire process of thinking is different. Some communities have business in their blood like - Guajarati, Marwari, Sindhi, Agarwals etc. They do business and flourish because they think differently. Hence for Self- Employment you need to think differently. No one can snatch your thoughts away from you. You need to have an entrepreneurial mindset.

Once it is decided to take up self-employment we need a proper entrepreneurial environment to convert that dream into a reality. He or she may also need hand holding so that they can proceed in the right direction and take guidance from expert people in that business. Adequate training is required so that the rural woman can run the venture smoothly. Hence training organizations play a significant role to upskill and develop the skills. The next thing which comes in the picture is the financial aspect as to how to raise funds. There are various ways through which funds can be raised and rural women can use the same to start-up their own entrepreneurial ventures.

Now we are at the final stage where everything is already done and now we are at the stage of giving a legal status to the venture. To give a legal status to the venture and finally start its operations requires lots to documentation and legal process are required which is stated in this book.

– Dr. Abhishek Mukherjee

About the Book

RURAL WOMEN – THE UNTAPPED POTENTIAL

"Rural Women: The Untapped Potential" is a book focused on budding entrepreneurs, students pursuing Management Education, Commerce students and Management professionals who are inclined towards entrepreneurship and planning to have their own startups in the near future. This book is an effort to exhume the hidden potential which exists in Rural Women of India with special emphasis on Maharashtra. This book reveals the various employment avenues extant in the Rural Areas which if tapped and used optimally can do wonders. The book covers various chapters like Job Vs Business, Entrepreneurial Mindset, Entrepreneurial Environment, Self-Employment Avenues – Sectors of Employment, Skill Analysis, Hand holding, Training Requirements and Avenues, Self-Analysis, Legal Procedures involved in establishing one's own startup, how to raise Funds etc. Thus this book tries to cover all the areas which are required to be tapped so that the women especially the rural women can be made 'Atma Nirbhar' (Self-Dependent).

This book includes various live examples of rural women entrepreneurship and also brings to light what steps rural women should take to generate self-employment.

Key Features

It covers all the areas which have to be taken into consideration when planning for a new startup.

The language used in this book is quite lucid which makes the reader very easy to understand the concepts and examples.

Explores the gap existing in the system because of which there are lots of hurdles and impediments in the way of entrepreneurship.

It explores the various sectors where self-employment can be taken up which will not only uplift the villages but also will make them self-reliant and will add to the progress of the country.

Coverage and Structure

The entire Book is divided in 10 different chapters. Each chapter deals with a specific aspect which needs to be addressed while planning for starting your own business and pursuing entrepreneurship. The chapters are not only from a rural woman's self-employment perspective but also applicable to people, students and youth looking forward towards entrepreneurship and starting their own venture or start-up through self-employment.

Chapter 1 introduces to the reader with Self-Analysis. It describes in detail what is self- analysis all about and discusses its need and importance. It further elaborates on how self-analysis can be done.

Chapter 2 addresses Skill Analysis and explains what is a Skill all about. It describes the various types of Skills and describes about skill analysis. The chapter discusses about the need and importance of skill analysis. The method to analyze one's own skills is explained in detail. This is followed by the explanation of how to convert the skill into a profession.

Chapter 3 is devoted to the Difference between Job and Self-Employment. It talks about what is employment and how is it different from a job. The difference between employment and self-employment is also discussed. The need and importance of self-employment is discussed followed by the various forms of self-employment. The comparative analysis between job and self-employment is detailed.

Chapter 4 describes the essence of Entrepreneurial Mindset. It describes what is an entrepreneurial mindset and how an entrepreneurial mindset is different. The chapter further describes about the characteristics of entrepreneurial mindset and discusses in detail the factors leading to an entrepreneurial mindset. It further describes about creativity and innovation and exhumes the positive results of an entrepreneurial mindset.

Chapter 5 exhumes the various Self-Employment avenues identified for Rural Women, Urban Women and Semi-Urban Women. The chapter further describes how to avail these self-employment avenues for entrepreneurship. The various factors influencing rural women towards entrepreneurship is described in detail. This is followed by the discussion on various challenges faced by rural women in using self-employment avenues and use her untapped potential.

Chapter 6 discusses the impact of entrepreneurial environment on the entrepreneurial venture creation. It talks about the Entrepreneurial Environment. It further details why an entrepreneurial environment is needed and is important. The chapter further describes how an entrepreneurial environment can be created. Creation of Entrepreneurial Environment has several positive impact and leads to creativity and innovation.

Chapter 7 talks about the importance of Hand Holding. It describes what is hand holding and why it is at all required for a rural woman entrepreneur. How will hand holding help her in creating her entrepreneurial start-up. The chapter further explains why hand-holding is important and how will it benefit the rural woman entrepreneur in self-employment.

Chapter 8 deals with the Training Requirements and Avenues. It details about the importance of training and its impact on the work or skill development. It further describes about the identification of training needs and areas where practical training is required. The various training institutes available for practical training for youth and rural woman is discussed along with the courses they can take up. The financial assistance provided by government under various schemes is also described to support and motivate youth and rural women towards self-employment and entrepreneurship.

Chapter 9 details about How to raise funds? It talks about the various ways in which funds can be raised by rural women to start their own venture. The identification of funds requirement together with areas in which funds will be required is also explained in detail. The various sources of raising the funds is also described and discussed in the chapter.

Chapter 10 describes about the steps taken to Establish the Start-Up. It details about the various legal formalities and registrations required to give a legal identity to the start up. Beyond providing a legal identity the various areas like infrastructure, work force, website creation etc., it also talks about the brand creation. It further explains the various steps taken to promote the venture and launching of the venture or the start-up.

Acknowledgements

Writing a book is a dream come true. I never thought in my wildest of the dreams that I will ever write a book. During my research journey while pursuing my Ph.D., when I visited the Rural Areas of Pune talked and interacted with Rural Women and confronted the reality, I actually felt that I should pen down all my experiences and share it with the world so that people who don't know about the villages and hidden potential should be made aware about the same. This motivated me to write this book.

First and foremost, I would like to thank all the rural women and all the rural women entrepreneurs whom I met during my research journey for cooperating with me, interacting with me and providing necessary information relevant to my Ph.D. research "A Study of Perception of Rural Women about Self-Employment and Entrepreneurial Opportunities."

Secondly, I would like to thank all my students who have inspired me to write this book and who can definitely utilize this book for their learning.

Thirdly, I am thankful and grateful to my loving wife Mrs. Shweta Abhishek Mukherjee who always stood by me as and when required and always supported and motivated me, because of which I could write this book.

My sincere thanks to my parents Shri Bratindranath Mukherjee and Smt. Jayati Mukherjee, as it is because of them whatever I am today. I am also grateful to my sister Smt. Shubhra Chakraborty, brother-in-law Mr. Neelanjan Chakraborty and my cute nephew Mr. Syon Chakraborty for their unrelenting help and support.

I extend my heartfelt thanks to my father-in-law Shri Debabrata Bhattacharya and mother-in-law Smt. Ratana Bhattacharya for showering their blessing and good wishes on me.

Fourthly, I would like to thank Mr. Saurav Bhowmik for motivating me and guiding me while writing this book.

My sincere thanks to Dr. Devendra Bhave Sir and Smt. Madhuri Bhave Madam for always supporting me and guiding me in life.

Last but not the least I would like to thank the entire team of Notion Press for continuously supporting me, guiding me from time to time and helping me in totality to publish this maiden book of mine.

About the Author

Dr. Abhishek Mukherjee

Dr. Abhishek Mukherjee is Assistant Professor and Program Head for MBA International Business Program at MIT World Peace University, School of Management (PG) at Kothrud, Paud Road, Pune. He has done his Doctor of Philosophy in Faculty of Commerce, Business Administration from Savitribai Phule Pune University, Pune, Maharashtra. His doctoral thesis is on 'A Study of Perception of Rural Women about Self-Employment and Entrepreneurial Opportunities'. He holds a Master's Degree in Business Administration and is UGC NET in Management. He also holds an M.Phil. Degree. He has a teaching experience of 14 years and an industry experience of 3.5 Years. He has published and presented 16 research papers in various

State, National and International Level Conferences and in various Journals. His subject areas of interest include Business Statistics, International Business, Business Research Methods, Research Methodology, Economic Analysis for Business Decisions, Managerial Economics, Business Communication, Soft Skills, Business Policy and Strategic Management, Marketing Management, Marketing Research, Services Marketing, Geopolitics & World Economic System and Entrepreneurship.

CHAPTER 1
Self-Analysis

बुरा जो देखन मैं चला, बुरा न मिलिया कोय
जो दिल खोजा आपना, मुझसे बुरा न कोय।

When I went out searching for bad people, I couldn't find anyone bad. The moment I tried to introspect and see my own heart, I found no one bad than my own self.

Learning Objectives:

- To understand what is Self-Analysis?
- Determine the need and importance of Self-Analysis.
- To develop the ability to do Self-Analysis.
- To understand the Step by Step Procedure to do Self Analysis.

Learning Outcome:

- Will be able to do Self Analysis
- Ability to understand the need and importance of Self-Analysis
- Do One's Own Self Analysis
- To understand how self-analysis can help in future growth.

Chapter Outline:

1. Self-Analysis:

1.1 Introduction

1.2 Self-Analysis

1.3 Need for Self Analysis

1.4 Importance of Self-Analysis

1.5 How to do Self-Analysis?

Summary

1.1 Introduction:

I often ask this to my students that if Lata Mangeshkar Ji, (Nightingale of India) would have gone for playing cricket and Sachin Tendulkar, world famous cricketer, would have gone for singing Classical Music, what would have happened? It would have been disastrous. They would never have achieved success which they have achieved now. Hence it becomes imperative to understand our own self.

We often talk about neighbors, our relatives, cousins, friends, colleagues, enemies etc. and know a lot about them. We try to seek entire knowledge about them. What is happening in the neighbor's house, who is having affair with whom? Who ran away with whose fiancée? How many marks Sharma Ji's Son scored in 10th Standard? What is happening in your cousin's family? We have complete knowledge about all this. But if someone asks to write about your own self then it becomes difficult. In an interview, if the interviewer asks that tell me something about your own self then we fumble. We are not able to speak about our own self. Knowing your own self is very important. We spend maximum amount of time with our own self. We remain with our own self for about 24 hours in a day. But still we don't know our own self. Have you ever tried to ask these questions to your own self?

Who am I?

Why have I come on this earth?

What is the purpose of my life?

What are my qualities, my talents?

What are the things I am good at?

Out of these four things, which is the thing which I can do the best?

Do people really know me and my talent?

Have I ever tried to exhume my potential to others?

Have you ever met people who have the same talent which you have?

What steps have I taken to develop my talent or my inherent capabilities?

Which specialization should I choose?

Which course should I choose?

What job should I do which will lead to success?

Which vocation to choose which will yield more money?

A very few of us actually do this. Every decision is taken by others, even starting from your own name. Our name is also decided by others and not by yourself. May be your parents or your aunt or your granny or some other relative might have decided your name.

This approach is very wrong. People just compare us with others and say, Mr. X, son of Sharma Ji did this and now he is earning a huge amount of money, he has achieved success but you could not do so even after I spending so much money on you. It seems as if we are in a rat race. Often the parents don't understand that every child is different and has unique talents and skills. Hence it is futile to compare my son with other's sons or daughters. It is not mandatory to do what others are doing. We need to understand this. It is very important to understand that we all are different and everyone is unique. God has bestowed every one of us with some or the other talent. But due to lack of awareness, lack of proper counseling, proper training, whom to approach for counseling and guidance the entire talent goes for a toss. By the time you are able to analyze all these things it is too late.

1.2 Self-Analysis:

Self-Analysis is a way or we can say a method of analyzing one's own self and try to figure out our own talents and competencies. It is basically SWOT analysis of one's own self. It will help us to understand that what am I good at? It is often seen that people who are academically not very good are still able to earn a good amount of money in spite of not having a very sound academic background. Thus it gets clear that, though formal education is important but it is not mandatory that it will definitely lead to more money. Self-analysis helps us to understand what am I meant for. It is important to understand that we cannot be proficient in everything or every field. But one can be excellent in some areas may be sports, music, dance, elocution, writing etc. Today we can make our career in any of the fields because there are plethora of opportunities and avenues available.

God has blessed each one of us with some or the other talent. But it is very important to first analyze our own self and analyze our area of interest. You all might have seen the movie Lion King. If a lion starts living with other animals, over a period of time he forgets that he is lion and starts behaving like another animal. In the same way if you fail to determine your competency and start blindly following others then you will never be able to achieve success. You will have to compromise. Many a time it happens that we want to do something, we wanted to become something but finally end up became something else. By the time we are able to realize and do self-analysis it is too late. Hence self-analysis needs to be done at the right time.

1.3 Need for Self Analysis:

I have seen many engineers who have done engineering. After pursuing engineering for three years they realize that engineering is not their cup of tea. But then they cannot go back and finally are compelled to complete engineering. After completing engineering when they don't get a suitable job, they go for higher studies like MBA etc. then may finally get a job in a Bank and sit in the teller counter, collect and count cash or do a job of selling credit and debit cards or a sales job of opening savings bank accounts of customers. Now how will this person utilize the skills which he learnt in the engineering program. This is a criminal wastage of time, energy and money. Engineering skills are not required to work in a bank to count money. This has happened because we want to copy others without knowing and analyzing what are we meant for.

There is a huge need for self-analysis. We need to understand, what am I meant for. Every job requires a specific kind of skill. Every person cannot do every job. For example, for Marketing jobs you need to be street smart, with excellent communication skill in multiple languages and not mere English. He or she needs to be an extrovert as you will have to talk to the customers are sell your products and services. You should be ready to travel across and meet customers even during night hours or as per the availability of customers. Beyond this the person should have negotiation and convincing skills. He or she will have to work under pressure, moreover the job is also target oriented. The salaries are high with some component of fixed salary and some incentive based salary. If you want to earn incentives, you will have to perform and show results. More over if you have a big EGO then you are misfit for a Marketing job because then you will not be able to sell your products and services in the Market. You need to be very polite and humble while talking to and dealing with customers and should have the knack as to how to make a deal. Marketing people are the bread earners of the company because these people go to the field and reach the final end customers and bring money to the organization and generate revenue for the organization. If a person doesn't have fluent communication skills, if you are shy and looking forward for an arm chair job then you are misfit for marketing jobs.

Similarly, for Human Resources Management Jobs, you require a different skill altogether. You need to be patient and have to be calm and composed. If a group of agitated workers or employees come to you in your cabin, you will have to listen to them and understand their problem in place of shouting and arguing with them. You need to do the competency mapping of individual employees and understand their training needs and how can these employees be developed in the organization. Recruiting the right kind of candidate for the right job, understanding his or her training needs based on the profile, doing a gap analysis, and upskilling the employees by providing suitable training is the work of HR employees and Managers. Thus people who are very arrogant and short tempered are not fit for this kind of jobs.

If we talk about Finance jobs, they require good calculation skills and you should have good numerical ability to do such jobs. If you are not good in Mathematics and hate calculations etc., then you are not fit for Finance related jobs. Thus in a nut shell it is very important to understand the area of our interest. If we are not interested in a particular area but still keep on doing the same as we are forced to do the same out of compulsion, then we will do it somehow but will never enjoy the work. It is very important to understand that every person is different and has different skills, competencies and talents. It is again based on the individual's level of education, family background, level of parents' education, maternal and paternal side, genetic characteristics etc. Every person is meant for a particular kind of work as per the talent and skill, but very few of us actually get the opportunity to do the right thing at the right time because of the absence of a proper guide, mentor or a well-wisher.

In the context of Rural Women, the scenario is again different. The level of education is different, but they have more practical knowledge. During my research I found that women who are illiterate and have never undergone any formal education are also able to run their business because they have learnt doing business practically. They know the basics like currency, how to count money, how to do farming etc. because they have done these things practically themselves and not just merely reading books. Every woman is unique and is pursuing a different kind of business. Family background also plays a vital role.

1.4 Importance of Self Analysis:

Self-Analysis is important because once you have done this, you will be able to enjoy the work you like to do. Otherwise your work will become a burden for you. Whether you like it or you don't like it, you will have to do it because **"Paapi Peth Ka Sawal"**. Nobody will feed you for your entire life. We all need to understand this. Your parents, friends, relatives, colleagues etc. can support you to a certain extent but then finally it is your life. You will have to knead your own dough.

Once you are able to determine what are you passionate about and do the same, then work will not become a burden. Rather you will enjoy doing your work day and night without any complain. Money will definitely come. But very few of us do this. We see what others are doing, what have they done and started earning so much of money. In-spite of doing so much why am I not able to make so much money which my other friends, colleagues, cousins, relatives have done and are minting money now. There is a difference and we need to accept that. There is a difference in the approach and thought process. Mr. Shiv Khera in his Book Titled – 'You Can Win' has very aptly written that winners don't do different things; they do things differently.

Self-Analysis can do wonders as you can now focus on your inherent capabilities and develop them. Once you become self-aware and starting investing your energy and money on yourself to work on your skills and abilities under proper guidance of a mentor or a Guru the life really changes. Guru or Mentor plays a significant role in one's life as he or she may guide us choosing the right path to achieve pinnacle of success. Google cannot help you always. It is definitely a source of information but a Guru or Mentor has a significant role as he or she will be able to guide you what needs to be done and what is not required to be done.

1.5 How to do Self-Analysis?

Skill analysis is very important for an individual failing which we may land into a vocation which may not interest us but are compelled to continue with as we are not left with any other option. Hence doing self-analysis at the right time and finding a mentor or guide at the right time can do wonders to an individual. Don't follow others, follow your own self. Do your own self-analysis. Sit, try and introspect, what are the three to four things I am good at. Once you do an introspection and understand what am I good at, start working in the same lines. Ask these questions to your own self:

What are the various areas of my interest?

How can I develop on those areas?

Who are the people who are already there is those areas?

What do they do?

How do they work?

How have they developed and converted their passion into a vocation?

What challenges have they undergone?

How have they established their business from a scratch?

How can I go and meet those people?

Try to go and meet those people and interact with them.

Learn from their experiences, talk to them and ask questions to them.

Ask for the potential avenues as to how can you groom yourself.

What sought of a training is required to enter into that vocation?

From where can I get that training?

Summary:

The chapter discusses about Self-Analysis and its importance. As each one of us is different and are unique, bestowed with different competencies and skills. Every one of us is capable, but differently. But sometimes it happens that we are not aware of what we are capable of and hence self-analysis becomes important. Self-Analysis deals with analyzing oneself in terms of one's areas of interest and what are we capable of. It is very important to do self-analysis as that will help us to follow the right path in our career. We need to understand what are we meant for? Are we doing what are we meant for or simply compromising in doing something trivial that is not our cup of tea.

The chapter further describes the need of self-analysis and how it is important for any individual. Self-analysis is important as it is a kind of eye-opener which will help us understand our own abilities and capabilities. This will help us to utilize our skills and talent in the right direction and will further develop those inherent skills. Self-analysis exhumes the area of our interest and provides us an idea what are we passionate about. If we choose a vocation of our own choice and not as a compulsion, then we will enjoy doing our job as we are passionate about it. Otherwise we will do a job as we need to feed ourselves and family but not enjoy the job.

The chapter further describes a step by step approach as how to do self-analysis. This will not only provide the right direction in decision making to follow a suitable career path but also help us achieving success in that career as the skills required for that particular will be properly mapped. Hence we can understand how self-analysis can do wonders in an individual's life and can help us achieve pinnacle of success.

******

Chapter 2
Skill Analysis

कस्तुरी कुंडल बसै,मृग ढूढ़ै वन माहि
ऐसे घट घट राम हैं,दुनिया देखे नाहि।

"The fragrance of musk is there in the navel of the musk deer, but the deer being unaware of that keeps on searching for the fragrance from pillar to post. In the same way Lord Ram is everywhere but people are unable to see Lord Ram. The same happens with we human beings, the skill is inherent in our own self but we are unable to understand and keep on going from person to person to give us knowledge about our skills."

Learning Objectives:

- To understand What is a Skill?
- To understand the various types of Skills.
- To explain What is Skill Analysis?
- To determine the need and Importance of Skill Analysis.
- To explain how to analyze one's own skill?

Learning Outcomes:

- To determine one's own skill.
- To analyze the various types of Skills.

- To incorporate Skill Analysis
- To discover the Need and Importance of Skill Analysis.
- To relate with one's own skill

Chapter Outline:
2. Skills Analysis:

2.1 Introduction

2.2 What is a Skill?

2.3 Types of Skill

2.4 What is Skill Analysis?

2.5 Need and Importance of Skill Analysis

2.6 How to analyze one's own skills?

2.7 How to convert your own skills into a vocation?

Summary

2.1 Introduction:

The word 'Education' has a Latin origin and is derived from a word "Educare" which means 'to nourish', 'to bring up' or 'to raise something'. The traditional Indian Education system was entirely practical and application oriented. In the ancient times, we had the Varna System where in the society was divided into 4 Varnas, Brahmin, Kshatriya, Vaishya and Shudras. "Brahmins" used to impart education to the society, "Kshatriya" were basically warriors and soldiers. We had the "Vaishya" who were business men and finally the "Shudras". In Ramayana and Mahabharata also we have studied and seen in various serials telecasted on television that we had the "Gurukul System". We have also read about the "Ashram System". The society had a proper structure. There were four Ashrams – "Bramhacharya Ashram", "Grihastha Ashram", "Vanprastha Ashram" and "Sanyas Ashram". The students used to go to the "Gurukul" wherein they were admitted. They used to go for the "Bramhacharya Ashram". It was a residential program. They used to stay in the Gurukul with the Guru (Rishi Muni) and Guru Ma. The Guru used to teach the students and impart knowledge under a tree. The classes were conducted in an open environment and the method of teaching and learning was through storytelling and practical application. The Guru used to impart practical knowledge, for example archery, horse riding, swimming, doing various domestic chores etc. practically. The entire administration and functioning of the Ashram was taken care by the Guru and his students. Even the exams conducted were very practical. It was all skill based. There was no fixed curriculum. After the completion of practical knowledge and training the students used to go for a bath, after which they used to be called "Snatak" (Graduate).

After becoming a "Snatak" the students used to go for "Grihastha Ashram" wherein they used to get married. But marriage was also skill based. There was a system of "Swayamvar" where the males or kings will have to prove their worth in front of everyone during "Swayamvar" and then only you will get a wife. The women were also given complete freedom to select their own husband who could meet the competency level as specified in the Swayamvar. Thus we can understand that skill was given due importance. You need to be skilled if you want to achieve pinnacle of success.

2.2 What is a Skill?

A skill is defined as an ability to do a particular task. God the almighty has bestowed all of us with some or the other skill be it human beings, animals or plants etc. Skill is the inherent capability of an individual to do certain things. Every one of us is blessed with some or the other skill. Singing, Painting, Dancing, Fishing, Swimming, Cycling, Boxing, Anchoring, Communicating, Running, Fighting, Orating, Acting, Weaving, Embroidery, Switching, Sewing, Writing, Convincing, Selling, Motivating, Learning, Cooking, Carpentry, teaching etc. are all various types of skills.

We can learn two things. First is how to eat fish and second is how to do fishing. If you just learn how to eat fish, then you will always be dependent on others. Because you will have to wait for someone to fish for you, cut it, cook it, garnish it and serve it on your platter. Then only you will be able to eat it. But once you learn fishing, any time you feel like eating fish, you can go for fishing, cut the fish, prepare the cuisine as per your palate and relish it. Unfortunately, the present education system is teaching us how to eat fish and not fishing. But it is very important for all of us to learn fishing so that we become independent and we won't have to look at people to show mercy on us.

Once you work on your skill, you can definitely convert your skill into a vocation of your own. Today's economy is entirely skill based where the application of knowledge is more important than just having knowledge. You may have plethora of knowledge but if you don't know the application of that knowledge, then such knowledge is futile.

2.3 Types of Skills:

The skills can be of various types which are described and discussed below:

2.3.1 Inherent Skills: These are those skills which an individual is born with or we can say genetically transmitted. We can say it is in the genes of an individual. For example: singing, dancing, acting etc. Some are born with such skills or talents.

2.3.2 Acquired Skills: These are the skills which can be learnt from a person who is proficient in that particular area. The people who have interest in that area can acquire such skills from the veteran person. For Example: Swimming can be learnt, cycling can be learnt, driving car can be learnt.

2.3.3 Hard Skills: These skills are basically technical in nature and hence called as Hard Skills. These skills are learned professionally and can be tested by incorporating suitable methods. These skills are used to do a specific kind of work or a task assigned to an individual. Example: Skills to handle a particular machine or equipment.

2.3.4 Soft Skills: Soft Skills may be defined as a combination of interpersonal skills, communication skills, social skills etc. which people show among others.

2.3.5 Conceptual Skills: These skills are usually required by the top level management people to take proper decisions. The top level management people have a high level of conceptual skills as it helps them in taking proper decisions for the organization.

2.3.6 Technical Skills: These skills are mainly required by people at lower level management who are at the floor level or the operational level. These skills are the skills which are used to operate a machines in the production unit.

2.3.7 Human Skills: People with such skills can easily connect to the audience. They are meant for social media and can do wonders for business purpose.

2.3.8 Life Skills: Life skills are the skills required to meet the demands and combat the challenges one gets in life. Example: Withstanding the challenges imposed on people by Corona Pandemic is an example of life skills.

2.3.9 Social Skills: Man is a social animal and as such has the skill of communicating and interacting with others. This inherent skill is called as Social Skill. Example: Being social in the society we live is an example of Social Skills.

2.3.10 Area/Domain Specific Skills: These are skills pertaining to a particular domain or area in order to perform or work in a particular profession. Example: Production Manager will require certain skills, Marketing Manager require certain skills like convincing skills, negotiation skills, selling skills etc.

2.4 What is Skill Analysis?

God the almighty has bestowed every one of us with some or the other inherent capability, talent or skill. Every one of us has got some or the other talent. But the need is to identify one's own talent, skill and work on the same. Develop the skill into a vocation.

Skill Analysis is the process of analyzing one's own capabilities and let people know what am I capable of doing. It is a way of introspecting into one's own self and understand about one's own capabilities and competencies.

2.5 Need and Importance of Skill Analysis:

The need and importance of skill analysis is very vital and significant. It is very important for all of us to understand that every person does not have every skill. But every person has some of the other skill. It is also important to understand that every person is not meant for every kind of job. Every job we do requires different skills set. Every person has a different interest. If you do what interests you, then you will definitely enjoy doing your work or job. The various points pertaining to the need and importance of skill analysis is discussed below:

2.5.1 Right Skill for the Right Job: Skill analysis will help us in mapping the right skill for the right job. When the right kind of person with necessary required skills is given the right task, the task will be accomplished soon as the person is already skilled to perform the task.

2.5.2 Will improve quality of work: The quality of work will improve which will lead to perfectionism. The person will do the task wholeheartedly and will complete the task without mistakes. As he or she will love doing the work of his or choice, the work done will be quality work as the person will give his or her heart and soul to do the work and complete the work.

2.5.3 Doing Job in short span of time: As the person employed to do the work has the right kind of skills and attitude, the work will be done in a very short span of time, without hassles. This will increase the efficiency of the organization also as a result of which more amount of work can be done in less amount of time.

2.5.4 Saves Time: When the work is performed by professionally trained people it saves a lot of time rather than giving the work to a novice who lacks professionalism. People with the right kind of skills and experience to do the work will give a professional touch to the work and will also minimize the errors which can happen if the same work is done by a novice.

2.5.5 Job will be done swiftly: By using the right kind of people with apposite skills for the job the organization will become agile. The person will swiftly complete the task assigned and bring different variations also in doing the same job. He or she can also provide us various different ways of doing the same job.

2.5.6 Bring Innovation in doing work: When a person is assigned a task he or she like to do or is good at, he or she can bring lot of innovation and creativity in doing the job. He or she can bring innovative ways of doing the same job. He or she can also suggest methods by which the work can be completed like a perfectionist in the shortest possible time.

2.6 *How to Analyze One's Own Skills?*

Only having skills is not sufficient. The problem most of us face is that, many of us don't know 'what skills do I have'? Even if we try to understand our skills, we don't know how can we use these inherent skills and start a venture of our own. Once we introspect and understand. I possess the following skills. It becomes imperative for us to understand that how can I convert my inherent skills into a vocation which will generate revenue and money throughout our life. How can I create and start my own venture? It is also important to understand what are the various industries or vocations where in my skills can be used and make myself self-sustainable by creating my own venture.

In order to analyze one's skills following steps needs to be adopted:

2.6.1 Self Introspection: Self-introspection will help you to understand your own true self. It will not only help you to do your own SWOT analysis by understanding your strengths and weaknesses but will also help you to understand your threats and challenges. This will provide a clarity to your pool of talents and skills.

2.6.2 What can I do with these skills of mine? The next point which comes to one's mind is that what should I do to utilize these skills of mine. How many people actually know that I possess these skills and how can I hone these skills. Your parents can help you at this very juncture as they have been fostering you and are aware of your capabilities. It may sometimes happen that parents are oblivious then someone else who likes you, loves you or observes you can give you a proper guidance.

2.6.3 How can I work on developing on those skills? It is very important to hone your skills. In order to hone your skills, you need the right ambience or environment. You need to meet the likeminded people as they only know the nuances of that particular field. Hence it is very important to get the right Guru. Sometimes, it may happen that your initial guru is your father or mother. Your brother or sister can also be your guru from whom you can learn primarily. Later you can approach a professional or a veteran to develop yourself professionally.

2.6.4 Bring Proficiency in that Skills: You need to be a champion in whatever you do and you should be known for that. You need to be a specialist and not a generalist. This can be brought by regular practice. You need to practice a lot in order to develop and bring refinement in your work. You should leave no stones unturned to keep on developing on your skills and keep learning to upskill your own self.

2.7 *How to Convert your Skills into a Vocation?*

One should always follow his or her passion. He or she should do a vocation of one's own choice and interest as we all are unique and have our own skill sets. A step by step approach to do self-analysis is discussed below which may help an individual to choose a vocation of one's own choice and excel in the career. This will not only make you happy but also generate money as you would be following your passion.

2.7.1 Identify the Skills that you have the best: Every one of us is bestowed with some or the other skills. Hence it is very important for an individual to identify those three four skills and pen down the same on a piece of paper. For Example: You may like sports, music, painting, dancing, etc. Try to identify three things you are best at.

2.7.2 Ranking the Skills: The ranking of the skills is very important based on your liking as well as acknowledgement from others. People should appreciate the talent you have when you have showcased them. For Example: If you do a lot of painting, show your work to others and get your art work displayed and have a genuine feedback from others. It will help you to get a clear picture.

2.7.3 Analyze whether those skills are inherent or acquired: Analyze whether the area of interest you have shown or are pursuing is an inherent quality or you have acquired as it interests you. If it is an inherent quality, then someone in your family might possess that quality and you may learn the same from him or her. If the skill is acquired, then try to practice and work on developing the skill from a Guru or a person proficient in that field. Join a proper class and take proper coaching from a professional at a very tender age.

2.7.4 Determine at what level the Skill is: Introspect yourself and analyze where do you stand? what are your deficiencies? and how to convert those weaknesses into strengths? Practice, practice and practice. Work hard to develop on your skills. Try to bring as much improvement as you can in your work.

2.7.5 Determine the ways to hone your skills: Get yourself professionally trained from a renounced School, College or University as this will bring a huge transformation and will further provide platform to learn new things, meet new people and opportunities for upskilling your own self. This will also give you lot of practical exposure and will develop confidence in yourself. More and more people will be aware about your skills.

2.7.6 Identify a Guru or an Industry Expert: You need to identify a Guru in the industry or an industry expert. Every one of us require a god father who will help us and bring us to light. A Guru will not only help you in professional development of your skill but will also introduce you to the industry and people associated with him, her or the institution.

2.7.7 Analyzing the Industry and the Opportunities in the Industry: When you start getting proper training from a Guru or under the guidance of an expert in that industry, he or she will do a lot of handholding and will provide platforms to showcase your talent and skill. Beyond this you should also search for opportunities to show your skill and talent to others in the industry. You will have to do lot of networking with people, talk to people and develop relations. Because this will help in getting more opportunities as you will have contacts.

2.7.8 Use AIDA Model: Here you need to use the Attention-Interest-Desire-Action Model which is popularly known as AIDA Model. Pounce on the opportunities to show your skills and grab attention of people. People should know you for your work and skills and they should be interested to collaborate with you for learning from you. They should desire to work with you or get associated with you. Finally, this will lead to action and people will start calling you at several events and occasions. This will open doors for more opportunities and generate money. Now once you achieve recognition, you can charge for your own work and generate money.

2.7.9 Start Generating Revenue and Money: Once your skills and work are liked by people they will definitely have to pay in order to acquire a product or a service of yours. Hence now you will start generating revenue for your skills and work. Now your skills have been converted into a revenue generated profession. As there is no free lunch, people will pay to get the work done from you.

2.7.10 Start your Own Venture: Now is the time to start your own venture as now people know you in the market and in the industry. People know well what are you into what is the quality of work you do. Hence now once you start your own venture, you can run it successfully. Only starting your venture is not sufficient. You will have to work continuously, add new products, services into your new venture. Keep meeting new people, develop on your network. Keep learning new things. Try to promote your venture at various platforms, and grab opportunity to provide visibility of your venture. Keep organizing various events, seminars, webinars to create awareness amongst the people.

Summary:

The present chapter deals with Skills and Skill Analysis. It describes what is skill all about? Skill is the ability to perform a particular task. It is discussed that how our earlier education system was skill based. How the entire learning was skill based which was very practical in nature? More emphasis was given on the application of the knowledge and how the skills were used to get the work done. The chapter further details about the various types of skills like – Inherent Skills, Acquired Skills, Hard Skills, Soft Skills, Conceptual Skills, Technical Skills, Human Skills, Life Skills, Social Skills and Area or Domain Specific Skills. The chapter also explains the need and importance of Skill Analysis and how skill mapping helps in getting and right kind of vocation for oneself. It also explains how to analyze one's own skills. The step by step approach is explained to understand how skill analysis can be done. The chapter also explains the steps to convert your skill into a profession of your own choice and how it can help in creating your own venture. Venture creation of your own, based on your skill analysis will not only provide self-employment and self-sustainability but will also open doors of employment for others who can join and contribute to your venture. The same concepts are applicable to rural woman using which she can go for self-employment based on her own skills thus creating and generating employment for others.

*****

CHAPTER 3
Employment Vs Self-Employment

लक्ष्यमेकं तु निश्चित्य तत्रिकाग्रं मनः कुरु
सैयमेन् कृतो आभ्यासह शीघ्रं सिद्धिं प्रय्यछति

"It is very important to decide your aim first. Once the aim is set, then you need to concentrate your mind towards achieving the aim. If you keep on regularly practicing towards achieving your aim with patience, you will speedily get success."

Learning Objectives:

- To define Employment.
- To explain the term Employment.
- To discuss what is a Job?
- To compare the various types of Jobs
- To determine what is Self-Employment?
- To compare between Job Vs Self-Employment

Learning Outcomes:

- To explain what is Employment.
- To describe the term Employment.
- To discuss what is a Job.
- To identify the various types of Jobs
- To explain what is Self-Employment?
- To differentiate between Job Vs Self-Employment

Chapter Outline:
3. Employment Vs Self Employment:

3.1 Introduction

3.2 Employment – Meaning and Definition

3.3 What is a Job?

3.4 Self-Employment

3.5 Forms of Self-Employment

3.6 Need for Self Employment

3.7 Importance of Self-Employment

3.8 Comparative Analysis of Job and Self-Employment

Summary

3.1 Introduction:

In order to survive on this earth, we need food, clothing and shelter. These are the basic needs of any human being in order to survive on this earth. We need food to satisfy our hunger, clothing to cover our body and shelter to prevent ourselves from rain and dust, thunderstorm and wild animals etc. But human beings are not satisfied with basic needs. We all have different wants. Wants are defined as desire for specific products. Then comes the demand, which is the desire for a specific product backed by the willingness to pay for it, ability to pay for it and the availability of the product or the service.

In order to have a good life and satisfy our demands we all need money. Money is not God but also not less than God. In today's scenario, everywhere, we first need money to get anything done or availing anything, starting from food, clothing, shelter to all the necessaries and luxuries of life. Even for maintaining relationships money is required. In order to earn money, we need an employment or a job or we can also go for self-employment. We are all taught to be a good human being but are not taught how to earn more money. Money can be earned from various ways, which may be ethical or unethical. But at the very outset it is very important to decide what I actually want to do? Whether I want to work for myself and earn a lot of money or I want to get employed somewhere else into a job and earn money. Hence a proper planning is very much important at the very starting of one's career that what one actually wants. Once this gets clear, then steps can be taken accordingly.

The same is applicable in the context of Rural Woman also. She needs to decide whether she wants to go for employment somewhere or is looking for avenues for self-employment based on her inherent skills.

3.2 Employment – Meaning and Definition:

Employment can be defined as a legal engagement of rendering your services to an organization or employer, under certain terms and conditions, through certain designations and doing a job or an assigned task by which an individual earns money in the form of wages or salaries and makes a livelihood.

3.3 What is a Job?

A job is basically a task or an assignment given to an individual under employment for which he or she will be paid for in order to earn his or her livelihood. The employer gives the job to an employee under certain legal terms and conditions mentioned in the appointment letter in which the employee will have to perform. The employer will remunerate the employee for the work done by the employee as per the terms and conditions decided during employment.

3.4 Self-Employment:

Self-Employment is an act of engaging oneself in an activity based on the skills inherent in oneself and creating a product or service of your own choice as per the societal needs and providing the same to people and thereby earning money through profits in return. In self-employment you are your own boss and are governed by your own terms and conditions.

3.5 Forms of Self Employment:

In a developing country like India and in many other developing countries, there are various forms of self-employment by which by individuals can earn their livelihood. These are as follows:

3.5.1 Home Based Workers:

Home based workers are those who produce products such as bidis, garments, textiles, footwear, food products and handicrafts either on their own as artisans or on a piece rate from a contractor or middleman.

3.5.2 Small Petty Traders, Vendors, and Hawkers:

Small Petty Traders, Vendors and Hawkers are those who sell household goods or vegetables, fruits, eggs, fish and other food in market place or move with a head load or a push cart from village to village or in the streets.

3.5.3 Provider of Services and Manual Labour:

Provider of Services and Manual Labour are those self-employed people who are engaged in agriculture, construction, transportation, cleaning, laundering, health, catering or domestic help.

3.6 Need for Self-Employment:

Self-Employment is the need of the hour. In a developing country like India, every year lakhs of engineers, doctors, MBAs etc. are coming out of Engineering colleges, Medical Colleges and Top Notch B Schools. If we see from the point of view of an Economist, the demand is less and supply is more. The rate at which these professionals are coming out from various universities and colleges the number of industries are not growing or getting established at the same pace. Hence the supply is more and demand is less. This is leading to under employment if not unemployment. Because then students or professionals will have to compromise on the pay package because if you don't take up a job someone else will take up. Hence it is of vital importance that the young generation creates jobs rather than seek for jobs. India now needs job providers rather than job seekers.

The same is applicable to rural areas also. The rural youths migrate to urban areas because of lack of opportunities available in rural areas. After coming to urban areas they face cut-throat competition as the supply of quality work force is more. As rural youth is not able to compete with people in urban areas they are compelled to go back to rural areas again. This leads to frustration and this frustration gets converted into domestic violence in the family and children. The woman in the family and children become victims. Hence self-employment of youth in the village as well as self-employment of rural women is of utmost importance and is the need of the hour.

3.7 Importance of Self-Employment:

Self-Employment has immense potential. Hence youth should definitely explore for self-employment opportunities as per their skills and talent. By undergoing self-employment under proper guidance and mentoring youth can convert their dream into reality.

The various areas which makes describes the importance of self-employment are stated as under:

3.7.1 Opens Employment Opportunities for Others:

Self-Employment leads to the creation of Start-Ups or one's own venture. This not only benefits the entrepreneur or the individual who took the initiative to start his or her own venture but also benefits others in the long run. It creates employment avenues for several other who are like minded and come together and work. Rural women as well who want to start their own venture and go for self-employment will not only be generating revenue from the same but will also open doors for so many rural women who are like minded and want to become financially independent.

3.7.2 Makes oneself Self-Sustainable:

Self-Employment makes an individual self-sustainable. He or she won't have to beg for jobs, but is now in a position to generate employment and give jobs. The entrepreneur is not a job creator and reduced the chances of unemployment. By this action he or she is standing on his or her own foot and will not have to live on the mercy of others. By becoming an entrepreneur, he or she work can generate revenue and profits. Profits can be invested and the entrepreneur can further go for expansion of the venture. The same is applicable to rural women once they become self-employed and become entrepreneurs. Thus rural women become self-sustainable in the long run and will not have to be dependent on others.

3.7.3 Development of Society:

Self-Employment not only leads to self-development but also leads to the development of the society in the long run. Self-Employment generates plethora of employment opportunities for people living in the society. This in turn leads to revenue generation or cash flow. When cash flow takes place people in the society become financially more strong. They become more independent and this leads to the development of the society as well because now people are able to afford which they could not afford because of paucity of money.

3.7.4 Uplifts Standard of Living:

Self-Employment leads to money generation. When money flows in then we don't just adhere to the basic necessaries but also try to meet our wants. Because of paucity of money rural women used to compromise and were meeting only basic needs. But after creating ventures of their own, they are now able to generate more amount of money and revenue which they can now spend on other activities and spend on converting their dreams into reality. Money or cash flow uplifts the standard of living of rural woman and now she can have a better life with financial security.

3.7.5 Provides Work Life Balance:

By starting her own venture rural woman can work from home and won't have to wander here and there in search of employment. By working from home she can not only take care of her start-up but at the same time take care of her children, husband, parents-in-law and other members of the family. Thus she is able to strike a proper work life balance. She can spend quality time with her family as well as devote time to her own venture as well.

3.7.6 Platform for Future Generations:

Once the Start-Up is established and nurtured properly with complete devotion, it will definitely generate revenue for generations. Hence it is a long term investment. It is often said as you sow, so you reap. It may take time to launch a start-up as it requires a lot of planning to do the same. But once a start-up or a new venture starts, family members, people gradually start getting involved in the business. The current generation also involve their children who also get practical learning. Thus the next generation gets an established platform, because when you start doing your business, you develop, contacts, networks, you come to know about the market, suppliers, customers, competitors and so many things which adds to your knowledge. This relations work in the long run and can be carried forward for generations. Thus once a start-up is launched by a rural woman it can become a platform for future generations as well.

3.7.7 No Retirement:

When you do a job, you will have to retire or you may have to leave the organization any time if you are not able to meet the expectations of your boss or employer. But entrepreneurs never retire. Once you have your venture, you will never retire. You can go on expanding your business, locally, nationally across different states, and finally across to one country or several countries. Thus you will never retire or perish off unless and until you stop learning and continuously upskilling yourself. It is very important for an entrepreneur to keep abreast with the latest technology, and updating oneself continuously. The same is applicable to rural women entrepreneurs also. Starting a venture is not sufficient. Rather you will have to keep on learning and adding new products, services and facilities in order to survive in the market.

3.7.8 More Growth Opportunities:

There is plethora of opportunities for growth in self-employment against going for a job. When you are employed and doing a job, your growth is restricted. Your growth depends on your Boss or your supervisor or on your employer. Sometimes even if you work, your work may not be highlighted. It does not come into limelight and hence you are not acknowledged and suitably rewarded. But when you are an entrepreneur and have your own Start-Up, setup then sky is the limit. No one can control you, no one can restrict you from doing things for your own or for your own venture. You are free to work and definitely returns will come to you. This also happens because now you don't look into your watch for time. You just are passionate about your work and keep on doing it. Rural women also have more growth opportunities when they become self-employed and take up entrepreneurship. Because now the remote control of their life is in their own hands.

3.8 Comparative Analysis of Job and Self-Employment

S. No.	Job	Self-Employment
Points of Difference		
1	Job is like a rented house where in you are the tenant.	Self-Employment is like you are the owner of the house.
2	Here you are an employee.	Here you are an employer.
3	You will have to work as per the needs and wants of employer.	You need to have a clarity about your work you are going to do.
4	Your employer or your boss is the decision maker.	You are the decision maker of your own destiny.
5	In a Job your responsibilities are limited to your own self.	When you become an entrepreneur you will have to be more responsible.
6	Your progress is limited and is dependent on the mercy of the employer or boss.	Your progress depends on your own self and the hard work you put in.
7	Challenges / Risks are limited as you are just an employee.	Challenges / Risks are more as your employees are entirely dependent on you.
8	You are feeding your own family.	So many families are dependent on you and your enterprise.
9	You can change your job.	You can diversify your business.
10	Roles are limited	You need to play several roles.
11	Salary is limited, you get limited money at the end of the month.	You get money based on the efforts you put in. More efforts you put in more money you can generate. No efforts no money.
12	You cannot take leaves as per your wish. You need approvals from your Boss.	Any time you can take a leave and go for a vacation.

S. No.	Job	Self-Employment
13	Mood Based Salary. The disbursement of Salary is very erratic, keeps on changing based on the mood of the employer.	You need to generate money and pay salaries to your employees.
14	Regular updation is required but depends on the job profile.	Every time you need to be updated and upgraded in order to survive in the market.
15	Less freedom of work.	More freedom of work.
16	You have a supervisor to supervise you.	You are your own supervisor.
17	Minute to minute planning is not that required as the final planning is already done by the employer. You are just an executer and not a planner.	You need to be meticulous and should do a proper planning in terms of annual plans, monthly plans, weekly plans, daily plans, hourly plans and minute to minute plan.
18	You search for an opportunity.	You create an opportunity.
19	For anything and everything you are answerable to your boss.	You are answerable to your own self or to the stake holders.
20	Capital is not yours, it is provided by the employer.	Capital is either your own or else you have raised the capital.

Summary:

The chapter discusses the difference between "Employment and Self-Employment". It is very important for an individual at the very outset that what he or she wants to do. Whether one wants to go for employment and go for a job, or one wants to start his or her own venture and undergo Self-Employment. The various terminologies like employment, job and various types of self-employment are discussed which an individual or rural women can take up. The various types of self-employment opportunities like home based workers, petty shop traders, vendors and hawkers, providers of service and manual labour are discussed. The need and importance of self-employment is discussed pointing out the various ways in which it can help the women entrepreneur. Why is self-employment essential in today's competitive environment and how can it benefit an individual who wants to become an entrepreneur and create his or her own venture is elaborated. The chapter also explains various points of difference in detail between job and self-employment. This comparative analysis also helps in taking a proper decision which can really benefit an individual in the long run.

******

Chapter 4
Entrepreneurial Mindset

सर्वं परवशं दुःखं सर्वमात्मवशं सुखम्।
एतद् विद्यात् समासेन लक्षणं सुखदुःखयोः॥

Everything which is other's control leads to pain and unhappiness. Everything that is within self-control leads to pleasure and happiness. This is what pain and happiness means.

"Once a man asked a Honey Bee – You make a lot of honey and then we men come and take away all your honey. Don't you feel bad about it? The honey bee answered: I don't feel bad because you are only taking my honey, but the art of making honey still remains with me. Hence even if you take away all my honey I can again make honey as I have all the skill to make honey".

Learning Objectives:

- To understand what is entrepreneurial mindset?
- To analyze how entrepreneurial mindset is different?
- To discuss the factors leading to entrepreneurial mindset.
- To elaborate on creativity and innovation.
- To explain the positive results of entrepreneurial mindset.

Learning Outcomes:

- To explain what is entrepreneurial mindset.
- To describe the difference between entrepreneurial mindset and others.
- To discover the factors leading to entrepreneurial mindset.
- To explain creativity and innovation.
- To identify the positive results of entrepreneurial mindset.

Chapter Outline:
4. Entrepreneurial Mindset:

4.1 Introduction

4.2 What is Entrepreneurial Mindset?

4.3 How Entrepreneurial Mindset is different?

4.4 Characteristics of Entrepreneurial Mindset

4.5 Factors leading to Entrepreneurial Mindset

4.6 Creativity and Innovation

4.7 Positive Results of Entrepreneurial Mindset

Summary

4.1 Introduction:

Have you ever thought that why can't all of us become Entrepreneurs? Usually it is seen that after completing education students take up job and start working in a company with a lucrative salary. Only few of them don't take up a job but rather think of establishing their own venture. They feel that they should have their own company or they should do something of their own and establish a Start-Up or a New Venture. They have a mindset of "Be Your Own Boss". The only difference which makes these students different from others is their mindset. Similar things happen with rural women also. Not all of them have the ability to start their own venture. Only few of them have the craving of doing something of their own and starting their own Start-Up which will not only help them to become Self-Employed but also open doors for several others to get employment. Thus it is the Entrepreneurial Mindset which makes all the difference.

4.2 What is Entrepreneurial Mindset?

An Entrepreneurial Mindset points out ways of thinking about business opportunities and leverage the same by extracting benefits from uncertainties. "Entrepreneurial Mindset" is a tendency of the mind or ability of the mind to think in a creative manner or critical thinking. Entrepreneurial mindset is associated with self-competence or self-capability. An entrepreneurial mindset not only deals with self-capability but also with various other factors like creative thinking, one's experience, one's knowledge, opportunity seeking capability, problem solving approach, one's attitude, beliefs etc. Thus people with entrepreneurial mindset have a creative bend of mind. They have the ability of critical thinking which makes them different from other people.

4.3 How Entrepreneurial Mindset is Different?

Entrepreneurial mindset comes from the field of psychology. Entrepreneurial mindset particularly deals with Personality Psychology. The entrepreneurial mindset is associated with an individual's thinking ability. People with entrepreneurial mindset look for opportunities instead of obstacles, look forward to provide solutions to problems instead of making complaints. Thus, it can be understood that people with entrepreneurial mindset find opportunity in every problem and try to make maximum from it rather than cribbing, crying and counting the problems. In a nutshell, people with entrepreneurial mindset are solution providers rather than problem creators.

4.4 Characteristics of Entrepreneurial Mindset:

People with entrepreneurial mindset are different from others. Entrepreneurs have entrepreneurial mindset hence they can see things which non-entrepreneurs cannot see. The same is applicable to rural women as well who have entrepreneurial mindset. They can see opportunity is every challenge and hence are different. The various characteristics of an entrepreneurial mindset are mentioned below:

4.4.1 Passionate about exploring new opportunities:

Individuals with entrepreneurial mindset are always passionate about exploring new opportunities. We can say they can also create opportunities. Such individuals are always alert and look forward towards ways of making profit from the changes and disruptions happening in the business world or the way they do business.

4.4.2 Highly disciplined in pursuing opportunities:

People or individuals with such mindset not tap the opportunities meticulously but also record the unexploited opportunities which has not been tapped yet. They act on these unexploited opportunities if they find them to be feasible and attractive. They leave no stones unturned to pursue the opportunities with zeal and zest.

4.4.3 Pursue Only the Best Opportunities:

This means that entrepreneurial mindset people don't move here and there for tapping every opportunity. They analyze the opportunity and target only those opportunities which have better results. Thus by doing this they focus their energy and efforts on selected opportunities which will provide maximum benefit or yield.

4.4.4 Focus on Execution:

The focus is more on execution of the opportunity. Definitely they can change directions if they get something more during the execution of the opportunity, while exploring new opportunities as well. Hence execution of opportunity is given more importance and people with entrepreneurial mindset focus on the same.

4.4.5 Domain Centric Energy Engagement:

Domain centric energy engagement means individuals are able to maintain good network and sustain good relationship with people both within and outside the business. Thus emphasis is on building a good network and relationship with people who are directly or indirectly related to the business and sustaining the same.

4.5 Factors Leading to Entrepreneurial Mindset:

There are several factors which develops entrepreneurial mindset or entrepreneurial thinking. The factors leading to creation of an entrepreneurial mindset is mentioned below:

4.5.1 Family Background: It is often found that some communities are very entrepreneurial or business oriented like Guajarati, Marwari, Agarwals, Sindhi Communities. Business is in their blood. The best thing in them is that they give practical exposure to their kids from a very early age. Kids after school hours or college hours go and work and support in their dad's business. They are not oriented to do a job or service.

Hence the family background makes a lot of difference.

4.5.2 Entrepreneurial Environment: The entrepreneurial environment in the family also creates a lot of impact. When children in the family listen to their parents talking of starting their own venture or doing something of their own. They too get motivated and think in the same direction. Once they see things practically happening in front of their eyes how a venture is coming into existence, how their parents are working day and night to establish their venture. They also gradually get involved if parents share the same with their kinds in the family.

4.5.3 Training: Before starting your own venture it is very important to undergo practical training. This will be an eye opener. Because there is a lot of difference between bookish knowledge and practical knowledge. For example: If you want to start your own medical store. First you need to fit in the eligibility and the qualification required to start your own medical store. Then you need to get a license for the same. Beyond this, before starting your own setup or venture, you should go and work in a medical store so that you will practically understand how things happen in real life even after acquiring required qualification and degree. This will help you to understand the system more properly. Thus a proper training also creates an entrepreneurial mindset and we start thinking differently.

4.5.4 Education and Learning: Doing something without knowing, and doing the same thing after acquiring a proper knowledge about it makes a lot of difference. For example: There are so many people who sing and sing well. But they don't know what are they singing? Which Raga are they singing? What are the notes? etc. Now when a person who wants to take up singing as a career, learns music from a professional singer, he or she gets educated and learns the nuances of singing. Thus education and leaning also opens up the entrepreneurial mindset.

4.5.5 Work Experience: Work experience develops entrepreneurial mindset. Once you work and gain experience. Your brain opens up and you find different ways of doing things through your experience. Your experience of doing things makes you more confident as now you know what all things can be done. Experience makes you more confident and prevents you from taking wrong decisions. Thus your experience creates an entrepreneurial mindset and encourages you to think differently.

4.5.6 Risk Taking Ability: The risk taking capability boosts entrepreneurial mindset. When we have already taken a risk and done an investment, we need to think from an entrepreneur's perspective towards all the dimensions associated. This will also compel the individual to think from an entrepreneurial mindset that how can we generate profits and revenue. Thus the entrepreneurial mindset again helps and individual to take up more risk. Finally, we need to understand that an entrepreneurial mindset can only see opportunities and motivate an individual to take calculated risks.

4.6 Creativity and Innovation:

Entrepreneurial Mindset leads to creativity and innovation. People with entrepreneurial mindset have a very creative bend of mind. They are always looking for new things or think of creating something new. Creativity leads to innovation. Innovation leads to opening doors to plethora of opportunities. Thus with the help of creativity and innovation lots of employment opportunities and self-employment opportunities gets created. People with entrepreneurial mindset with their skill of bringing newness or through innovation generate employment which leads to revenue generation. Rural women with entrepreneurial mindset living in villages create avenues for others and their own self through creativity and innovation.

4.7 Positive Results of Entrepreneurial Mindset:

A healthy mind lives in a healthy body. If your thoughts are positive, then your body will also remain healthy. A person having entrepreneurial mindset also keeps on searching for opportunities or finds ways of creating opportunities. The positive results that are seen because of an entrepreneurial mindset are stated below:

4.7.1 Creation of Own Start-Up: Person with an entrepreneurial mindset will set up his or her own venture. He or she will not search for employment avenues but will create avenues for his or her own self of others. Self-employment and creation of one's own start-up will make them self-sustainable. The same is applicable to rural women with entrepreneurial mindset. They can generate self-employment and make themselves independent and self-sustainable.

4.7.2 Employment Generation: Creation of own venture will not only generate employment but will also generate employment for others. A venture cannot be handled independently and will require people and thus will open employment opportunities for others.

Employment opportunities can open for two people or two hundred people depends on the type and size of venture. If a rural woman opens a small venture of let's say tailoring she will be able to employ few more women. Thus this will lead to employment generation.

4.7.3 Extending Support to budding Entrepreneurs: An entrepreneur who has started his or her own venture is aware about the process of entrepreneurship. He or she can educate others and can bring awareness in the society. Thus they can provide assistance and support to budding entrepreneurs and help in creation of their venture. The assistance can be provided by the existing entrepreneurs to the budding entrepreneurs in terms of finding financial assistance, infrastructural assistance, human resource assistance and also providing contacts for legal and other assistance.

4.7.4 Creation of Entrepreneurial Environment: People with entrepreneurial mindset promote in creation of an entrepreneurial environment. An environment where in people can think out of the box and can do something extra ordinary. Creation of entrepreneurial environment supports other budding entrepreneurs to come forward with their own thoughts which can be given a proper shape and can be converted into a revenue generating Start-Up.

4.7.5 New Product Creation: When an entrepreneurial environment is created, people are encouraged towards creativity and innovation. Creativity and innovation promotes creation of new products. This can be done through ample amount of research and development. Thus rural women who have an entrepreneurial mindset can create and develop new products. This will help them to tap new markets and can lead to revenue generation. Thus regular efforts should be put in towards new product development.

4.7.6 Develop Risk Handling ability: An entrepreneurial mindset has a capability to see an opportunity even during unfavorable times or conditions. The people with such entrepreneurial mindset develop the ability to handle the risk. As such they don't get carried away the moment they see a risk. They know how to convert the risk into an opportunity. For example, the rural women in villages started making face masks during Covid 19 pandemic. This shows that they are not carried away by the risk but leveraged it to earn money and use the opportunity to do something innovative as per the need of the environment.

4.7.7 Emotional Stability: People with entrepreneurial mindset are emotionally stable. They are very practical and hence they think logically or rationally. They have developed how to cope up with challenges and because of this only they are emotionally stable. Emotional stability also brings maturity in them. They can take decisions be thinking or perceiving the things from all dimensions. Rural Women with entrepreneurial mind set also are emotionally stable. They think logically and rationally and have a practical approach towards their venture. This makes them emotionally more stable.

4.7.8 Challenges and Stress Handling: People with entrepreneurial mindset have the ability to cope with challenges and stress. As they have the potential to convert a challenge into an opportunity, they don't get stressed easily. The ability to convert a challenge into a opportunity makes them more confident. By confronting more and more challenges, they become so strong mentally that they don't get stressed any more. They know how to handle challenges and remain clam even in difficult times. Rural women with entrepreneurial mindset also have this potential. They remain calm and composed even during difficult times and not lose their cool. They search for avenues so that they can easily come out of grave circumstances.

Summary:

This chapter describes why all of us can't become entrepreneurs? There are few people who become entrepreneurs and there are people who go and work for those entrepreneurs. This happens because the people who want to become entrepreneurs are different. They think differently or we can say a different manner.

What makes them so different? The answer to this question is Entrepreneurial Mindset. "Entrepreneurial Mindset" is a tendency of the mind or ability of the mind to think in a creative manner or critical thinking. Entrepreneurial mindset is associated with self-competence or self-capability. An entrepreneurial mindset not only deals with self-capability but also with various other factors like creative thinking, one's experience, one's knowledge, opportunity seeking capability, problem solving approach, one's attitude, beliefs etc. The chapter further describes about how entrepreneurial mindset is different. It also elaborates on the characteristics of Entrepreneurial mindset. Further, the factors leading to entrepreneurial mindset is also discussed at length. How does entrepreneurial mindset create an impact on others is described by detailing about the positive results of entrepreneurial mindset? Suitable example of rural women with entrepreneurial mindset is given so that the students can learn from the same and are able to connect and understand how an entrepreneurial mindset can do wonders by opening plethora of opportunities for self-employment.

*****

CHAPTER 5
Self-Employment Avenues

कल्पयति येन वृत्तिं येन च लोके प्रशस्यते सद्भिः।
स गुणस्तेन च गुणिना रक्ष्यः संवर्धनीयश्च॥

The skill which gives sustainability to livelihoods and is appreciated by people, should be fostered and protected for one's own development or self-development.

"A bird sitting on the branch of a tree is never afraid of falling down from the tree. It is not because the tree is very strong. It is because the bird has confidence on itself and its wings. If the tree falls down the bird will fly and will go to another tree."

Learning Objectives:

- To understand various self-employment avenues available for Rural Women.
- To describe how rural women can avail those avenues of entrepreneurship and self-employment.
- To discuss the factors which motivate and support rural women towards pursuing entrepreneurship.
- To analyze various challenges faced by Rural Women while taking up self-employment and entrepreneurship.

Learning Outcomes:

- To discuss various self-employment avenues available to Rural Women.
- To explain ways by which rural women can avail those self-employment and entrepreneurship avenues.
- To determine the factors which motivates rural women for entrepreneurship.
- To discuss the challenges faced by Rural Women while taking up self-employment and entrepreneurship.

Chapter Outline:
5. Self-Employment Avenues:

5.1 Introduction

5.2 Self-Employment Avenues Identified for Rural Women

5.3 Self-Employment Avenues Identified for Women in Urban Areas

5.4 Self-Employment Avenues for Women in Semi-Urban Areas

5.5 How to avail the avenues of Self-Employment and Entrepreneurship?

5.6 Factors influencing Rural Women towards Entrepreneurship.

5.7 Challenges faced by Rural Women Entrepreneurs

Summary

5.1 Introduction:

"Rural Women – The Untapped Potential" is not just the title of the book but a reality. The women belonging to rural areas have huge potential which is still untapped. While doing my research in the rural areas of Pune and while visiting 13 talukas of Pune

Rural, it was found that rural women have immense potential and willingness to be self-dependent or we can say independent. They are very confident and are open to ideas of becoming independent. They want to stand on their own foot and become the bread earners of their family. They have a very positive perception towards self-employment. They want to take up self-employment and want to become "Atma Nirbhar". There is ample amount of support from family members and specially husband. Children are also supportive. The rural women are not highly educated but have the skills which can be used to develop them to become entrepreneurs. If proper guidance is given to them and awareness is created they can make them self-sustainable and will lead to income generation. There is plethora of avenues for rural women which they can take over and become an entrepreneur. The various self-employment avenues identified for Rural Women, Urban Women and Semi-Urban women is also described and discussed in this chapter ahead.

5.2 Self-Employment Avenues Identified for Rural Women:

Women participation in Rural Areas are found in the following fields: Agriculture, Horticulture, Sericulture, Dairying and Animal Husbandry, Fisheries, Home Based Industries like Handicrafts, Beedi Industry, Agarbatti Making (Incense Sticks), Tailoring and Garment Industry, Doll Making, Bee Keeping, Jewellery Making, Beauty Parlour, Printing, Textile, Food Processing, Nursery, Fashion Design, Baby Crèche Centre and Stationary etc.

Rural Women can also take up entrepreneurship in Agro based and allied products. There is huge scope of food, fruit and vegetable processing industry, Food preparation and processing as well. Many new markets have developed in the form of baby foods, ice cream, convenience food, cold drinks, canned products, traditional medicine preparation.

Picture 5.1: Self-Employment Avenues for Rural Women

Handmade Bags

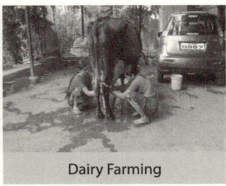
Dairy Farming

Cold Drink and Kokum Shop

Jewelry and Bangle Shop

Florist and Pooja Items

Tailoring Shop

Picture 5.2: Self-Employment Avenues for Rural Women

Picture 5.3: Self-Employment Avenues for Rural Women

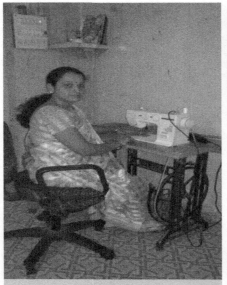
Switching & Fall and Pico Center

Nira Vikri Kendra

Broom Making

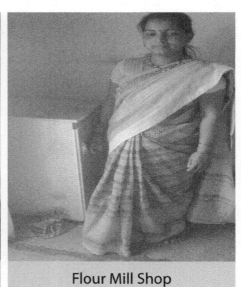
Flour Mill Shop

Picture 5.4: Self-Employment Avenues for Rural Women

5.3 Self-Employment Avenues Identified for Women in Urban Areas:

Urban areas being more developed due to industrialization and availability of technology and resources the avenues for Women Entrepreneurship are more and somewhat different. This is because here the women are given the opportunity to educate themselves and are more aware in comparison to women in rural areas.

The various entrepreneurial avenues for women in urban areas are: Computer Services and information dissemination, Trading of computer stationary, Computer maintenance, Travel and tourism, Quality testing, quality control laboratories, Sub-assemblies of electronic products, Nutrition clubs in schools and offices, Poster and indoor plant library, Recreation centers for old people, Culture centers, Screen printing, photography and video shooting, Stuffed soft toys, wooden toys, Mini laundry, community eating centers, Community kitchens, Job contracts for packaging of goods, Photocopying, Beauty Parlors, Communication centers like Cyber Cafes, etc. Other opportunities are Crèches, Catering Services, Tiffin Centers and Health clubs.

5.4 Self-Employment Avenues for Women in Semi – Urban Areas:

Women residing in Semi – Urban Areas have the following self-employment and entrepreneurship avenues: Production of liquid soap, soap powder, detergents, deodorants etc., Office stationary like cushion pads, gum and ink pads etc., Convenient, readymade, instant food products including pickles, spices, Papad etc., Community kitchens, Communication Services, Different types of training and coaching classes, Child Care Centers and Culture Centers for children, Nursery classes and Manufacturing of leather goods and Garments.

5.5 How to Avail the Avenues of Self-Employment and Entrepreneurship:

In order to avail the avenues of Self-Employment and Entrepreneurship, first and foremost it is very important to have the knowledge and awareness about the existence of such opportunity. In other words, we can say that, the rural women should be aware that such self-employment avenues at all exists. Before availing the self-employment avenues, the rural women should do self-analysis followed by skill analysis. This will help them to understand where do they fit in. By doing this they will also understand whether they have the entrepreneurial mindset and what are the various forms or ways through which they can go for self-employment. Beyond this, in order to avail the self-employment avenues, they should also have an entrepreneurial environment followed by a proper Guru, Guide or Mentor. This Guru, Guide or Mentor will do the handholding and will help in converting the dreams into a reality. They will also help and provide suitable guidance for getting trained and will provide suitable platforms for training. They will also help in providing proper information on avenues for getting or raising funds to start their own venture or start-up. Beyond this they will also assist in the formation of the start-up and its opening. Once the start-up becomes functional and starts working, they will also provide suitable support by monitoring the start-up and aid in its growth and development. Thus all the measures mentioned above can help rural women to avenues of self-employment and entrepreneurship.

5.6 Factors Influencing Rural Women towards Entrepreneurship:

Cooper (1985) identified three factors which influence entrepreneurship:

1. **Antecedent Influences:** These influences include family influences, stable dispositional factors that affect motivation, skill and knowledge.

2. **The Incubator Organization:** The nature of the organization where the entrepreneur was employed just prior to starting his/her business; the skills learned there.

3. **Environmental Factors**: The environmental factors deal with the factors which create entrepreneurial environment. The economic conditions, access to venture capital, support services and role model are some of the environmental factors which influence entrepreneurship.

Beyond this, it is rightly said the entrepreneurship is an activity which is situationally and culturally bound.

We can further categorize the factors influencing entrepreneurship into two i.e.:

1. **Pull Factors**
2. **Push Factors**

There are certain factors which allure and attract individuals towards them and as such the individuals get motivated and encouraged to take up entrepreneurship as a career. These factors are termed as **Pull Factors.** These factors pull the individuals towards entrepreneurship as the returns are high yielding and beneficial from future point of view.

On the other hand, there are certain factors which compel or force an individual to take up entrepreneurship as the individual is left with no other choice. These factors are circumstantial or situational factors under which the individual whether he or she likes or dislikes but takes up entrepreneurship as a career. These factors are thus the **Push Factors**.

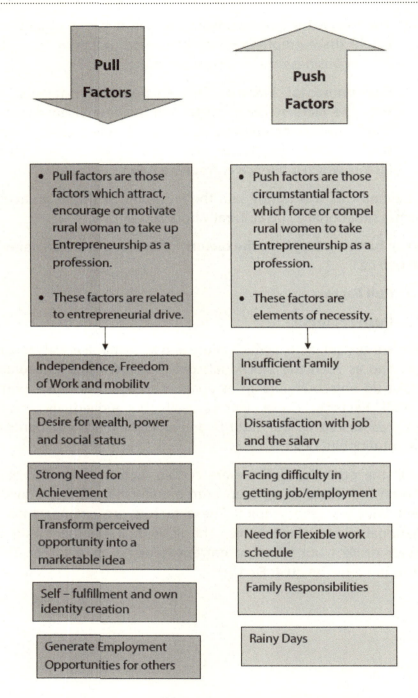

Figure: Factors Influencing Entrepreneurship

5.7 Challenges faced by Rural Women Entrepreneurs:

Figure: Challenges Faced by Rural Women Entrepreneurs

Rural Women have huge untapped entrepreneurial potential which if utilized optimally can do wonders to the society. Women if encouraged to become an entrepreneur can become the backbone of the family and make the family more self-sustainable. These would in turn also curb brain drain and migration to urban areas in search of jobs for employment. Rural women entrepreneur can herself generate employment and can open plethora of opportunities for other women as well. But there are several constraints which act as impediment and obstruct the path of women entrepreneurs from making them a successful entrepreneur.

Some of the challenges faced by Rural Women Entrepreneurs are as follows:

5.7.1 Finance Shortage: Women entrepreneurs suffer a lot in meeting the financial needs of the business and that of raising funds. Bankers, creditors and various financial institutions are not coming in front to support and provide financial assistance to the women borrowers. They think that women entrepreneurs are less credit worthy and have more chances of business failure. Women entrepreneurs also face financial problem due to blockage of funds in purchase of raw materials, work in progress and finished goods and non-receipt of payments from the customers for the goods they have purchased.

5.7.2 Raw Material Shortage: Non availability of raw materials or scarcity of funds acts as a disaster for the enterprise run by women entrepreneurs. Procurement of raw materials and its supply for production as and when required is a tough task for women entrepreneurs. It becomes more difficult when the required raw material available in the market is less is quantity and women entrepreneurs have to pay a higher price than normal to arrange for the raw material.

5.7.3 Fierce Competition: Women entrepreneurs have to face a tough cut throat competition in order to survive in an organized market with more male counterparts. They have to struggle very hard as the women entrepreneurs have low technology equipments for their production process. Male entrepreneurs being more experienced and having capacity to adopt advanced technology act as threat to Rural Women Entrepreneurs.

5.7.4 High Production Cost: High cost of production is another problem which reduces the efficiency and restricts the development of women owned enterprises. Women entrepreneurs face technological obsolescence due to non-adoption or slow adoption of changing technology, this in turn increases the production cost.

5.7.5 Dual Responsibilities: Women shoulder dual responsibilities both at the home front and at the professional front. Maintaining a work life balance becomes a tough task. For women as family comes first and is the priority sometimes she is not able to concentrate in the professional front even if she wants to do it and thus loses the opportunities. In India, it is considered women's duty to look after the children and other members of the family and thus involvement in the family leaves her with little time and energy for business.

5.7.6 Restricted Mobility: Women entrepreneurs confront the biggest problem of mobility. Travelling from place to place very often becomes a barrier for women entrepreneurs. Women entrepreneurs find it difficult to get an accommodation in the remote areas in smaller towns and this becomes a problem for them even if she wants to do something significant. Inability to drive vehicle also acts as a constraint which acts as deterrent to mobility. Moving alone in the night and asking for room to stay out in the night hours for business purposes is looked upon suspiciously.

5.7.7 Social Constraint: Indian culture and tradition acts as a barrier for rural women to take up entrepreneurship as a career. In rural areas, women have to face resistance not only from the husbands and other males in the family but also from the other elderly females who have accepted inequality. The attitude and perception of people in the society in which she lives acts as a barrier and restricts her growth and prosperity.

5.7.8 Marketing and Sale Constraint: Another major challenge which the rural women entrepreneurs face is the problem of marketing and sales of the products she has manufactured. Due to lack of knowledge and exposure she is often cheated and is unable to reach the markets where she can get good returns and profits. Thus lack of information and experience acts as a deterrent in revenue generation.

5.7.9 Risk Bearing Ability: Women entrepreneurs have a low risk bearing capacity because they are financially not very strong. It is observed the even Banks and other financial institutions are reluctant to give them loans as they doubt on her ability to repay the loan. Thus she has to go with the limited financial resources she has and is bearing calculated risks.

5.7.10 Educational Constraint: Lack of education, exposure to the professional world and lack of experience acts as a major drawback in the field of entrepreneurship. Even today in India women is still considered as a burden to the family in rural areas. Most of the women in India are illiterate and those who are educated are provided with less or inadequate education partly due to poverty and partly due to their male counterpart in the family. They are just compelled to do with the domestic chores and then are married at a very early age. Due to lack of education and exposure, women who have entrepreneurial potential live in dark and thus remain unaware about the avenues for her development, the development of new technology, advanced methods of production, marketing, and various schemes run by government to support them and encourage them to flourish and become self-sustainable.

5.7.11 Low Need for Achievement: In India, right from the birth of a girl child, sexual discrimination is made in the families. Girl born in the family is taught about her role in life which inhibits her independence and achievement. In the absence of this need for achievement urge, only few women are able to become successful entrepreneurs. Because a high need for achievement, independence and autonomy is required to become a successful entrepreneur.

In addition to the above challenges, lack of family support, conservative thinking and mindset of the family and society, inadequate infrastructure facilities, insufficient accessibility towards information and information sources, shortage of power and technical know-how and unavailability to sufficient training and awareness programs etc have retarded the growth of rural women entrepreneurs in India.

Summary:

This chapter exhumes the crux of the book titled "Rural Women – The Untapped Potential" It reveals that rural women have huge potential which is untapped and needs to be tapped. The chapter details about all the avenues available to rural women in which she can participate and can create a venture of her own and become self-employed. Women participation in Rural Areas are found in the following fields: Agriculture, Horticulture, Sericulture, Dairying and Animal Husbandry, Fisheries, Home Based Industries like Handicrafts, Beedi Industry, Agarbatti Making (Incense Sticks), Tailoring and Garment Industry, Doll Making, Bee Keeping, Jewellery Making, Beauty Parlour, Printing, Textile, Food Processing, Nursery, Fashion Design, Baby Crèche Centre and Stationary etc. Rural Women can also take up entrepreneurship in Agro based and allied products. There is huge scope of food, fruit and vegetable processing industry, Food preparation and processing as well. Many new markets have developed in the form of baby foods, ice cream, convenience food, cold drinks, canned products, traditional medicine preparation.

The avenues of self-employment for urban women and semi-urban women is also discussed in detail. The chapter describes the ways in which rural women can avail the avenues of self-employment. It further details about the factors which influence entrepreneurship both- push and pull factors. The various challenges faced by rural women entrepreneurs while they proceed to establish their own start-up venture is also detailed and explained with the help of suitable diagram. Thus it is understood that Rural Women with huge potential given proper exposure and training can definitely do wonders and contribute to family, society, country and also to the world at large.

*****

CHAPTER 6
Entrepreneurial Environment

जो रहीम उत्तम प्रकृति, का करी सकत कुसंग,
चंदन विष व्यापत नहीं, लिपटत रहत भुजंग ॥

Negativity can't create an impact on good people or positive minded people. On the other hand, positive minded people create an environment which drives away negativity. It is in the same way as snakes with venom don't create an impact on sandal wood in spite of they staying on the sandal wood tree, rather the fragrance of sandal wood gets transferred to snakes.

Learning Objectives:
- To understand Entrepreneurial Environment
- To discuss the need for Entrepreneurial Environment
- To determine the importance of Entrepreneurial Environment
- To discuss how to create an Entrepreneurial Environment.
- To analyze the support system of the Entrepreneurial Environment.

Learning Outcomes:

- To develop the Entrepreneurial Environment.
- To describe the need for Entrepreneurial Environment
- To explain the importance of Entrepreneurial Environment.
- To incorporate and create an Entrepreneurial Environment.
- To develop a support system for Entrepreneurial Environment.

Chapter Outline:
6. Entrepreneurial Environment:

6.1 Introduction

6.2 What is Entrepreneurial Environment?

6.3 Need for Entrepreneurial Environment

6.4 Importance of Entrepreneurial Environment

6.5 Creation of Entrepreneurial Environment

6.6 Support System of Entrepreneurial Environment

Summary

6.1 Introduction:

It is often seen that many people could not flourish in spite of having several skills and talent. Some people have lot of skills and talent but could never get the platform or environment to showcase their talent. Hence the entire skill or talent goes for a toss and then finally gets confined to a dustbin. It is not only important to have a fertile seed but at the same time the land will also have to be fertile for the germination of the seed to take place. If a fertile seed is sown into an infertile land the seed will die without germination. The same thing happens to entrepreneurs as well. You can have several skills and talent. You may have the entrepreneurial intension or an inherent urge to become an entrepreneur but if there is no one to support or listen to you, then definitely you can never become an entrepreneur. If there is no one to understand your entrepreneurial mindset, the entrepreneur cannot progress or prosper in absence of entrepreneurial environment. Hence it is very important to understand the entrepreneurial environment as it creates a huge impact on transforming an individual into an entrepreneur.

Rural women also have ample amount of potential, skills and talent. But because of lack of exposure and entrepreneurial environment, they are not able to exhume their entrepreneurial skills. Hence entrepreneurial environment is of vital importance for any entrepreneur to grow.

6.2 What is Entrepreneurial Environment?

The term 'Entrepreneurial Environment' consists of two words – 'Entrepreneurial' and 'Environment'. The term 'Environment' can be defined as anything which surrounds an individual, and 'Entrepreneurial' means activities which encourages, motivates or drives a person to become an entrepreneur.

Thus 'Entrepreneurial Environment' can be understood as a sum total of socio-economic conditions, education and training, and availability of financial and non-financial support, and government policies etc. which leads to entrepreneurial development or birth of an entrepreneur.

From an external perspective, **entrepreneurial environment** can be defined as sum of the legal and institutional environment, market environment, financial environment, entrepreneurial infrastructure, cultural, economic, and political environments that individuals have and motivates them and creates an inner drive that encourages entrepreneurship.

6.3 Need for Entrepreneurial Environment:

Entrepreneurial Environment exerts significant influence on individuals to become entrepreneurs. The same is applicable to

Rural Women as well. Having skills is of utmost importance. But the environment in which these inherent skills can be developed is equally important. Example: If a rural woman wants to start her own venture of let's say beauty parlor, and approaches her husband and family for starting the venture. If the husband and family members straight away reject the proposal, then the entire dream of becoming an entrepreneur is shattered. Hence we can say that there should be an environment in the family of doing business. If there is family business, then the perception towards doing business will be different. Hence a proper entrepreneurial environment is the basic need for individuals to think as an entrepreneur.

6.4 Importance of Entrepreneurial Environment:

Entrepreneurial Environment is of vital importance as it creates or generates entrepreneurs. If a budding entrepreneur gets a proper environment or like-minded people whose thoughts are similar or think in the same direction, then it can work like a miracle. It may even happen that family members may oppose the budding entrepreneur because they themselves have not thought about this in their life. Hence they don't have any exposure. Hence it is of no use expecting support from people who don't have any experience in that field. Rather they will demotivate and distract you from your path.

When we get a proper entrepreneurial environment, we also get a mentor, a trainer or a guide who will not only listen to you, understand you but also help you by providing proper guidance. He or she as a mentor can also give you a proper direction or path to follow which can help in converting your dreams into a reality.

Entrepreneurial environment creates a very positive impact. For Example: In villages when rural women meet other like-minded women who have similar kind of skills, they can form groups and learn from each other. Women who are already having their own ventures, can motivate or encourage and bring awareness amongst other rural women who want to become entrepreneurs but a searching for proper guidance.

6.5 Creation of Entrepreneurial Environment:

Entrepreneurial Environment will help an entrepreneur to create his or her own start-up or venture. In a proper entrepreneurial environment, entrepreneurs will be able to speak their heart out and will be able to convert their ideas into a reality. Thus entrepreneurial environment will also provide a platform for meeting and discussing with likeminded people, networking with people and a platform to learn from people who are already entrepreneurs and running their ventures profitably.

Following are the steps mentioned below for creation of an entrepreneurial environment:

6.5.1 Creation of Incubation Centers / Entrepreneurship Cell: An entrepreneurial environment can be created by the inception of an Entrepreneurial Cell or Incubation Center. Formation of Incubation Center will help youth – men and women whether rural or urban and provide a platform to seek guidance and convert their dreams into a reality. Many a times there are people with huge aspirations, but non-availability of a proper platform in their nearby vicinity acts as an impediment in creation of their own entrepreneurial venture.

6.5.2 Running Awareness Programs on Entrepreneurship: To create an entrepreneurial environment, lots of awareness programs needs to be conducted so that people are made aware that how can they take up entrepreneurship and start their own venture rather than hunting for a job. Awareness programs will not only encourage people to take up self-employment but will also build confidence in them. This will help to understand what kind of ventures to start? How much fund will be required? Which Products to choose? Which markets to tap? Who are the customers? etc. Thus it will be an eye opener and will motivate people to take up self-employment and entrepreneurship.

6.5.3 Encouraging and Motivating People to come with Entrepreneurial Project Proposals: After attending the awareness program on entrepreneurship, people can come up with entrepreneurial project proposals. The entrepreneurial ideas can be converted into a proposal with all the details regarding industry, product, market, logistics, funds, customers etc. which can provide a panoramic view of the proposal. A detailed project proposal helps to proceed further as we can easily do the feasibility study of the project proposal.

6.5.4 Registration of the Entrepreneurial Project Proposal at the Incubation Center or Entrepreneurship Cell: After a detailed entrepreneurial project proposal is ready, it should be submitted to the entrepreneurship cell or the incubation center. The registration of the project proposal should be done at the incubation center along with paying the requisite fees. The entire project proposal along with the necessary documents should be submitted at the entrepreneurial Cell or Incubation Center.

6.5.5 Feasibility Study of the Proposed Entrepreneurial Venture: Once the Project Proposal is received along with required documents at the entrepreneurship cell or incubation center, it is given to the experts to scrutinize the projects and do a feasibility study. The experts do a thorough study of the project and give a feasibility study report, stating the missing links and tentative profits that will be generated.

6.5.6 Testing the Success of the Venture: The feasibility study report is shared with the person who submitted the entrepreneurial report and a one to one counseling session is conducted with him or her so that practical implementation can be discussed at length. After discussion, the person is asked to do a market testing survey to understand the results in a practical way. After the market survey reports are received and the reports are found to be good. The person is asked to proceed to set up the venture.

6.5.7 Assistance in Setting up the Venture: Based on feasibility study report and market survey reports the budding entrepreneur is given assistance in setting up the venture. The entire support is extended related to finding the suitable location, raising of funds, networking with people who will extend support to the establishment of the start-up. This assistance provided by the entrepreneurship center will reduce the challenges that the entrepreneur is going to face.

6.5.8 Provide Platform for Networking: The incubation center or the entrepreneurship cell will provide necessary data base required to network with the suppliers, customers, etc. which will help them in running their business and start-up successfully. Networking with various communities on various platforms will also help in creating awareness and visibility of the newly formed Start-Up.

6.5.9 Providing Financial Assistance & Support: The incubation center will also help in providing proper support in linking with the banks so that the budding entrepreneur can take the loan benefits from the bank. The banks which provide support and loan facilities under various government schemes under entrepreneurship development program can be used by the budding entrepreneur based on his or her eligibility.

6.5.10 Providing Infrastructural Assistance & Support: The incubation center or the entrepreneurship cell will also provide assistance in searching a suitable location for starting the venture or but also help in setting up the infrastructure for the same. This will reduce the burden of the budding entrepreneur as infrastructural assistance is provided. Hence he or she will not have to move here and there for searching for guidance.

6.5.11 Providing Legal Assistance & Support: The entrepreneurship cell or the incubation center will provide proper support and guidance in doing all the legal formalities and procedures in setting up the venture. The incubation center will help in undergoing all the legal procedures, starting from getting a lawyer to signing all the documents for setting up the venture. After the entire legal procedures are completed the newly formed venture now comes into existence in real form.

6.5.12 Setting Up of the Start-Up Venture: After the registration of the business and after all the work is done finally the startup is now ready for its operations. A formal inauguration is important so that people know about the startup. Proper promotion of the venture on various platforms is very important to create awareness about the start-up. Posters, leaflets, and other promotional material should be given to people and some promotional activities should also be planned where the customers can participate and get benefitted.

6.5.13 Monitoring and Supervising the Start-Up Venture Created: The start-up created with the support of the incubation center or the entrepreneurship cell is now working in full swing. But that is not sufficient. The venture should be monitored by the entrepreneurial cell or the incubation center to see whether the venture is generating required profits or not. Proper review and audit will be done by the incubation center to provide a proper direction to the venture. They will also be given proper guidance and strategy to be formulated leading to the growth of the venture followed by expansion.

6.5.14 Extending Support to the Start-Up as and when required: The start-up can tie up with the incubation center or the entrepreneurship cell so that the owner of the start-up can keep on getting guidance and upskill themselves as per the current scenario. It can also undergo short term trainings provided by the entrepreneurship cell or the incubation center so that the venture owners can get benefit of the same. Thus extending benefits to the already established start-ups which got established by the entrepreneurial cell or the incubation center will act as a two edged knife as both the parties will get benefitted.

6.6 Support System of Entrepreneurial Environment:

The support system for creation of an entrepreneurial environment is stated below:

6.6.1 The various components which can lead to support system are project planning and development departments, banks and financial institutions providing loans and other facilities of establishing start-up.

6.6.2 Organizations providing infrastructural support, lawyers and legal advisors providing legal support can also act as a support system of entrepreneurial environment.

6.6.3 Beyond this there are consultancies and placement agencies providing manpower as per the requirement.

6.6.4 There are various training organizations which provide quality training and make people ready for employment or we can also say self-employment.

6.6.5 Various government organizations also act as a support system in creation of entrepreneurial environment. This is because they motivate and encourage to participate and create their own ventures through MSME schemes etc.

Summary:

It is not only the skill inherent in an individual which matters but also the availability of proper environment and people who can understand the importance of those skills and help in developing those skills. Thus not only the entrepreneurial skills imbedded in an individual matter but also the entrepreneurial environment. The same is discussed in this chapter. At the outset, what is an entrepreneurial environment is discussed, followed by its need and importance at length. 'Entrepreneurial Environment' can be understood as a sum total of socio-economic conditions, education and training, and availability of financial and non-financial support, and government policies etc. which leads to entrepreneurial development or birth of an entrepreneur. The various factors which lead to the creation of entrepreneurial environment is also discussed in the chapter. The various baby steps that needs to be taken in order to create an entrepreneurial environment is also elaborated which can be meticulously followed by the budding entrepreneurs who are looking forward towards starting and setting up their own venture.

******

Chapter 7
Hand Holding

अन्नदानं परं दानं विद्यादानमतः परम् ।
अन्नेन क्षणिका तृप्ति र्यावज्जीवं च विद्यया ॥

Hand Holding can be of various types. If you donate grains it is considered good, but if you donate knowledge it is considered the best. Because if you donate grains the person will be able to feed himself for some time but if you teach him the skill of growing grains he will be able to feed himself throughout life.

Learning Objectives:
- To define what is hand holding?
- To discuss the need of hand holding.
- To explain the importance of hand holding.
- To discuss the benefits of hand holding.

Learning Outcomes:
- To describe what is hand holding?
- To explain the need for hand holding.
- To discuss the importance of hand holding.
- To analyze the benefits of hand holding.

Chapter Outline:
7. Hand Holding:

7.1 Introduction

7.2 What is Hand Holding?

7.3 Need and Importance of Hand Holding

7.4 How Hand Holding can be done?

7.5 Benefits of Hand Holding

Summary

7.1 Introduction:

Entrepreneurship is the need of the hour. It not only provides self-employment to an individual but also opens doors for several others. But only thinking about entrepreneurship is not sufficient. We have already read in the previous chapters that it requires an entrepreneurial mindset. Beyond this it also requires the ability to take risk. Higher the risk higher the return, lessor the risk, lessor is the return.

Many times it happens that a person wants to become an entrepreneur, but because of lack of proper guidance the person is not able to achieve what he wants or is not able to convert a dream into a reality. This usually happens because we are surrounded with people who don't have that entrepreneurial mindset to think beyond. As already mentioned in the previous chapter, a person with entrepreneurial mindset thinks differently. Hence he or she may find it out of place, if he or she discusses the venture ideas or thoughts with members of his or her family.

When we are not well and suffering from an ailment or disease we go to a doctor who is specialized in that area. This is because, it is the specialized doctor who can diagnose the ailment properly and treat us accordingly so that we get rid of the ailment or disease and get well soon. In the same way when a person has an entrepreneurial idea he or she needs to go to the right person at the right time so that he or she can diagnose the entrepreneurial intension and provide necessary guidance. This means we all need a mentor, a guide or a coach who will do hand holding.

7.2 What is Hand Holding?

Hand holding can be described as meeting those people who are seasoned and are experts in that area or venture or entrepreneurial project and can help us in each and every step. They will provide a proper counselling and will help us in reaching our entrepreneurial goal successfully.

In other words, we can say that hand holding is seeking proper guidance and direction from experts of that domain or industry who can provide necessary guidance.

7.3 Need and Importance of Hand Holding:

Suppose I want to go to Bangalore let's say on 21st May 2021 from Pune. The first and foremost the question which comes to my mind is why do I want to go to Bangalore. What is the purpose? Once the purpose is known – I want to go to Bangalore to attend an International Conference. The second question which comes to my mind is what are the various ways of transportation by which I can go to Bangalore. We have three options available – Roadways, Railways and Airways. Based on my cadre in the organization, my eligibility and designation, I come to know that I can go by flight. Then the next question which comes to mind is which Airlines to go for to travel to Bangalore? Once the Airlines is decided let's say 'Spice Jet' based on availability on that day. The next is which class in the Airlines – Economy Class or Business Class. Once it is decided that I am entitled for Economy Class, the tickets can be then booked for 21st May 2021 for flying to Bangalore.

The process does not end here. I will also have to plan how will I reach from my home to Pune Airport? Will I go by a Cab, an Auto or my own vehicle? I decided that I will go by Cab and accordingly booked the Cab as well. When all this minute and detailed planning is done along with a back-up plan then I can smoothly fly to Bangalore on 21st May 2021 and reach my destination as planned.

In the same way a hand holding is required so that we are given the right direction and the right path to choose which will lead to success. If there is not handholding, then too we can reach our destination but it will take a lot of time as we will learn by doing a lot of experiments and may be getting distracted from our path. Once we are distracted, or if we meet those people who don't have any knowledge about your domain area or start-up he or she will never understand the things and you won't be able to achieve success.

The same is applicable to rural women as well. Whenever a rural woman thinks of starting her own venture, she requires a lot of hand-holding. This hand-holding can be done by her husband if he is aware of the field in which the woman is looking forward to establish her venture, or it can be any other family member who can provide her proper guidance. If that is not possible, she should search for the right person who can understand what exactly she wants the venture to be and can then guide accordingly. The person who is going to do the hand-holding should be proficient in that vocation and must have adequate experience.

7.4 How Hand Holding can be done?

You need to approach the right kind of person with the right kind of required skills as far as hand-holding is concerned. The consultant or the counsellor should be seasoned and should have the required knowledge, expertise and experience to guide. Hand holding can be done by adopting the following steps:

7.4.1 Reading the Mindset: The hand-holding can be started by reading the mindset of the budding entrepreneur or the aspiring entrepreneur. It is very important to understand in detail what the entrepreneur wants to do, what has he or she planned and has in mind? How is he or she planning to move ahead? Once all these questions are answered, there is a clarity of mind. It is very important to have a clarity of mind; without which it is very difficult to move forward. Hence the first step is reading the mind and provide clarity of thoughts.

7.4.2 Providing Possible Avenues: The next step is to discuss the possible alternatives which can be availed or the possible avenues which the entrepreneur can go for. It is always beneficial to have a plan B ready as the only certainty is that there is a lot of uncertainty. The various avenues available based on the discussion can also open several doors which were never thought off. Hence face to face discussion along with several sittings provide much clarity. Decisions once taken are not reversible hence we need to discuss a lot before arriving at any concrete decision as it will have its own repercussions in the long run.

7.4.3 Selecting the Best Feasible Avenue: After a lot of discussion we can pen down three to four best feasible avenues on a priority basis which will help in taking it further. This will also help to work further in much detail as the entrepreneur will have a detailed understanding. Selecting the best avenue after a lot of scrutiny leads to success of the venture as the related associated risks are taken care of. Hence we can say we proceed with calculated risk which reduces the chances of failure of the venture to nil.

7.4.4 Creating awareness about the related opportunities and challenges: The person or the expert can give alternative ventures which can be set up if the current venture which is thought of does not seem feasible. The person expert will also help in doing the gap analysis and will help in finding the gaps and filling necessary gaps. He or she will also create awareness and will make us understand on the possible challenges associated with venture creation.

7.4.5 Preparations to overcome challenges: The mentor will also guide and will help in preparing for the challenges which you may confront while setting up the venture or on several other areas. The entrepreneur should be aware of the challenges well in advance which he or she may confront while setting up the venture or enroute. This will help in minimizing the associated risk.

7.4.6 Preparation for Plan B: It is always beneficial to have a plan B. We are definitely very confident with plan A. But if plan A does not work then we should be ready with plan B. As the market conditions are uncertain and the environment is full or risk and uncertainty it is always advisable to have Plan B. This will help in minimizing the risk, as we have not kept all the eggs in the same basket.

7.5 Benefits of Hand Holding:

It is always said that "Well Begun is Half Done". Hand holding can help an entrepreneur in leaps and bounds as he or she is able to have the complete panoramic view of his or her upcoming venture which he or she has only dreamt off. Hand holding will lead to confirmation of the formation of the venture as the entrepreneur is able to take calculated steps with certainty to reach his or her destination. This will create a royal road to success.

7.5.1 Clarity of Thoughts: Hand holding leads to clarity of thoughts. There remains no ambiguity on What has to be done? When it has to be done? How it has to be done? Who is supposed to do it? Where it has to be done? etc. When all these questions are answered the path becomes very clear to proceed forward and act accordingly. It is always said – Plan your work and Work your plan. A robust plan will make the execution much easier and will lead to a successful venture.

7.5.2 Clarity on the Venture: Through hand holding we get clarity what will be my venture all about and how am I starting. Entrepreneurship can be of any form- you can start as a manufacturer, you can start as a wholesaler, a retailer, a supplier, an agent, a middleman or a service provider. What will be the venture? Will it be a Real Venture or a Virtual Venture etc.? All these related queries get clarified at the very outset of the starting of the venture. A proper diagnosis and prognosis will help in making the venture prosperous.

7.5.3 Clarity of the Industry: There is no problem in seeking help from others and taking help from others. We need to understand that we are not omniscient and hence should always keep our doors open in order to learn from the right kind of source and person. Hand holding provides us guidance on the type of the industry we are planning to plunge into and the various areas we need to understand and take into consideration in order to prosper. Lack of knowledge and experience can act as an impediment to success. Hence hand-holding will provide clarity on each and every aspect. It will provide clarity on industry, product or service chosen, people associated, opportunities, challenges and the areas where we need to protect and prevent ourselves so that we are not cheated. It is very important to understand who is a well-wisher and who is wishing for us so that we fall in well.

7.5.4 Clarity on Project Planning and Development Support: Hand holding will help us in proper project planning and development. It will also let us know the areas where in support will be required. It will also enlighten us with the areas of development and provide necessary support for the same. The project needs to be foolproof so that there are no chances of failure.

7.5.5 Clarity on Financial Matters: The budding entrepreneur will get a clarity on the amount of fund initially required to create a start-up. He or she will also be able to acquire knowledge on the various sources of funds which he or she can avail for getting money. Thus preparations can be made in advance regarding arrangement of funds may be from own source or from Financial Institutions or Banks etc. This will help in providing the funds as and when required.

7.5.6 Clarity on Infrastructural Matters: The expert providing handholding in Infrastructural matters. He or she may provide assistance in selecting the right place or location for starting the business. The mentor will also guide regarding the basic infrastructural amenities which needs to be developed and created as per the type of venture to start with. They will also provide the cost associated with in developing the infrastructure. As the mentors or consultants also have contacts with various builders and commercial space providers they can assist you in getting a suitable place for the business to start as that place will have more visibility and will be conspicuous to the customers as well. Beyond this the social media presence and visibility is also of immense importance because in today's digital world most of the customers are available on various digital platforms like Facebook, Instagram, Twitter and Linked in.

7.5.7 Clarity on Legal Matters: Expert opinion will also help in finding a suitable lawyer and getting the Start-Up venture registered under the Shop Act. 2018. These days the registration can also be done online through https://shopactregistration.in/ website. The Shop Act 2018 gives a legal permission to run the business. It is basically a license to a business or a Start-Up Venture whether it is a provision store a beauty parlor or any other shop or a small hotel. Shop Act License is a must document to legally do a business in India. The average fees for getting a Shop Act Registration is Rs.1500/-

Summary:

The impact of hand holding in starting a venture or Start-Up is discussed at length in this chapter. This chapter details about what is hand-holding and why is it at all important. Hand holding can be described as meeting those people who are seasoned and are experts in that area or venture or entrepreneurial project and can help us in each and every step. They will provide a proper counselling and will help us in reaching our entrepreneurial goal successfully.

The chapter further describes how can hand-holding provide immense help and support to a budding entrepreneur. The same is applicable to rural woman if she is planning to start a venture of her own. The need and importance of hand holding is discussed at length to explain the readers how it can add value and make life simpler.

The chapter further provides direction as to how hand-holding can be done by reading the mindset, providing possible avenues, selecting the best feasible avenue, creating awareness about the related opportunities and challenges, preparations to overcome challenges and preparation of plan B. The various benefits of hand holding exercise is also elaborated as it provides clarity of thought, clarity on venture to be created, clarity of the industry and clarity on project planning and development. Hand holding also provides benefits through financial clarity, infrastructural clarity and clarity on legal matters.

******

CHAPTER 8
Training Requirements and Avenues

करत-करत अभ्यास के, जड़मति होत सुजान।
रसरी आवत जात तैं, सिल पर परत निसान।।

By regular practice a dumb person can also become a knowledgeable person, just as when a rope is regularly rubbed on the rock it creates a mark on the rock. This means that practice can do wonders.

Learning Objectives:

- To understand the training needs.
- To explore the areas where practical training is required.
- To discuss on the Institutes which impart training to Rural Women
- To analyze the courses which Rural Women can take up for Self-Employment.

Learning Outcomes:

- To discuss about the training needs
- To describe the areas where relevant practical training is required.

- To explain about the institutes imparting training to Rural Women.
- To discuss the various short term courses for Rural Women.

Chapter Outline:
8. Training Requirement Avenues:

8.1 Introduction

8.2 Identification of Training Needs

8.3 Areas in which Practical Training is Required

8.4 Institutes imparting Training to Rural Women

8.5 Short Term Courses for Rural Women

Summary

8.1 Introduction:

It is often seen that there are some people who sing songs and have learnt the same by either listening to radio or watching television. The same is applicable to dancers also. Some people love to dance and do the same by watching performance of others may be on television or any movie or even through YouTube Channel. This shows that the talent or skill is inherent but no proper guidance or we can say professional guidance. When you sing a song or play any instrument without learning it, you exactly don't know what are you singing, which Raga, which Taal etc. While playing instrument also you don't know what are you playing which notes etc. Hence, it is very important to undergo a proper training from a veteran person who is in this profession or a maestro. Once you undergo a proper training in music which may be singing, dancing or playing an instrument, you actually learn thoroughly and once you are professionally trained you know what are you singing or which dance form is it or which chords are you playing on the instrument.

Hence training plays a very vital role because you learn a lot when you actually do it on your own in your real life.

The same is applicable to rural women who want to become entrepreneurs. If a rural woman wants to open a tailoring shop or a boutique and wants to start her own business. Then in spite of her having a basic idea to stitch, she must go for a proper training and enroll herself for a proper course. The course can vary in tenure and will depend on what all she wants to learn. Training will not only provide her practical exposure but she will be able to practice and learn from her mistakes. When we enroll and undergo a training program we have someone who can guide us and provide us a right path and direction. Thus training changes the entire perception of the learner. Because it may happen we used to think it in this way but we may come to know that reality is entirely different after going through a proper training.

8.2 Identification of Training Needs:

Training is very important as it makes an individual ready to deliver the product or the service in a professional manner. The ambience of the training center also plays a very crucial role as it motivates the person to learn further. If the training center works like a simulator, then training the candidate becomes easy because the same thing can be applied in the actual real life. For Example: If someone wants to learn car driving and joins a driving school. Then initially the driving is taught using a simulator. Now once the candidate gets acquainted with the basics then he or she is taken to an actual car and then the practical training inside the car is given. Now practical training becomes easy as the trainee knows the basic things like accelerator, clutch and the gear. Thus it is very important to understand the need and importance of training.

Similar kind of training is also seen for students who are undergoing the Airhostess or Stewardship training. Their classrooms are designed in the shape of an aircraft and the training is imparted as if they are serving the customers inside the aircraft. This gives them a practical training and help them performing their tasks in a proficient manner when doing the same in an aircraft.

Similarly, if the rural woman is given a practical training she can get equipped and can implement the same in a better manner when she goes for her own entrepreneurial venture.

8.3 Areas in which Practical Training is Required:

Once the rural woman has decided to do her own business and become an entrepreneur, she is already clear what she wants to do and which business is she going to start. Now it becomes very important for her to identify the areas where training is required. For example: A rural woman wants to open a tiffin center and she knows basic cooking. But that is not sufficient because she is aware of only one style of cooking which she has been doing in her own house. But the customers are very different with different cultural backgrounds. Hence she will have to undergo a proper training to cook food for people with different cultures. Hence a proper training is again required. Thus it is understood that she doesn't require training to cook basic food but difference cuisines which are cooked in different cultures and communities. Thus by enrolling for different short term and long-term courses she will be able to understand in what areas she need to undergo training.

The area of training will vary from venture to venture. If the rural woman is into a trading venture the type of training will be different. If she is into manufacturing or something, then the training will be different.

In certain ventures, equipments are required for cutting, grating or may be washing and drying. In such cases women needs to be trained about the equipments as to how to operate the same, how to process the raw material into a finished good etc. Other areas of training can be related to packing or packaging, storage and delivering the product and providing the associated service. Training on maintaining the hygiene and cleanliness is also significant.

8.4 Institutes Imparting Training to Rural Women:

There are various institutes which impart training to youth both men and women so that they can develop their skills and become entrepreneur by taking up self-employment and creating her own venture. Some of them are listed below:

8.4.1 Nagarvasti Vikas Yojana Prashikshan Kendra:

Nagarvasti Vikas Yojana Prashikshan Kendra is run by Pune Municipal Corporation. It provides vocational training on various areas where in youth and rural women can also register and undergo professional training. There are a variety of courses, which can provide adequate skill to youth and women so that they can become entrepreneurs and take up self-employment.

8.4.2 Rural Self-Employment Training Institute:

Rural Self-Employment Training Institute (RSETI) provides quality training to below poverty line youth and equip them with proper skill training and skill upgradation. This institute is managed by Banks and Government of India and State Government are cooperating actively. The concept is based on Rural Development and Self-Employment Training Institute. Each Rural Self-Employment Training Institute should at least offer 30 to 40 Skill Development programs throughout a Financial Year. These skill development programs should be on various areas. These skill development programmes are of short duration and varies from 1 week to 6 weeks. Credit linkage facilities are provided by banks to start own entrepreneurial venture or start-up after successful completion of the course.

8.4.3 Entrepreneurial Development Training Programme:

Ministry of Micro, Small and Medium Enterprises under the scheme of Entrepreneurship Skill Development programme (ESDP) regularly keep on organizing for youth and other people who are looking forward to set-up their own entrepreneurial venture or start-up. ITIs, technical institutes/business schools, and polytechnic institutes also organize such training programs for youth (men and women) with skills and talent and motivate them for self-employment.

8.4.4 Women and Child Welfare Scheme:

Pune Municipal Corporation through its women and child welfare scheme provide vocational training for women, self-employment training and Entrepreneurship Development Program for women. These programs help rural women is skill development and help in making them self-sustainable through self-employment.

8.5 Short Term Courses for Rural Women:

From the various available sources through secondary research and personal visit, the various short term courses provided by various institutes for Self-Employment for youth and Women are mentioned below:

8.5.1 Nagarvasti Vikas Yojana Prashikshan Kendra:

Various courses run by Pune Municipal Corporation under the Nagarvasti Vikas Yojana Prashikshan Kendra is mentioned below:

Nagarvasti Vikas Yojna Prashikshan Kendra

Pune Municipal Corporation

S. No.	Subject of Training	Minimum Eligibility	Course Duration (Month)
1	Mobile Repair	10th Pass	6 Months
2	Photography, Video Shooting and Photo Lamination	9th Pass	6 Months
3	Advanced Course - Color Photography and Color Processing, Digital Photography (Basic Photography Training Mandatory)	9th Pass	3 Months
4	Wiring, Motor Rewinding and Electric Equipments repairing	5th Pass	6 Months

S. No.	Subject of Training	Minimum Eligibility	Course Duration (Month)
5	Refrigerator, Air Conditioner Repairing	8th Pass	6 Months
6	Television Repairing	9th Pass	6 Months
7	Tally (Basic Computer Knowledge)	12th Pass	2 Months
8	MS CIT (More Practical Facility)	10th Pass	3 Months
9	CC++ (Basic knowledge of C Language) (Qualified entrance exam)	12th Pass	3 Months
10	Computer Hardware	10th Pass	7 Months
11	Computer Basics Training	9th Pass	3 Months
12	D.T.P (Basic knowledge of Computers required)	12th Pass	3 Months
13	V.B. (Basic knowledge of Computers/ Qualified Entrance Exam required)	12th Pass	3 Months
14	Oracle (C++ & Visual Basic qualified Certification mandatory)	12th Pass	3 Months
15	.NET (C++ & Visual Basic qualified Certification mandatory)	12th Pass	3 Months
16	JAVA (C++ & Visual Basic qualified Certification mandatory)	12th Pass	3 Months
17	AUTOCAD (Computer Basic knowledge mandatory)	12th Pass	3 Months
18	LINUX (Computer Hardware Basic requirement)	12th Pass	3 Months
19	Two Wheeler Repairing	4th Fail	6 Months
20	Fashion Designing / Embroidery (Basic Stitching Training required)	8th Pass	6/2 Months
21	Screen Printing	Literate	2 Months
22	Gardening	Literate	6 Months
23	Solar Energy Equipments repairing	9th Pass	3 Months
24	Leather Purses and Bags	Literate	6 Months

S. No.	Subject of Training	Minimum Eligibility	Course Duration (Month)
25	Fur Toys & Soft Toys	Literate	6 Months
26	Beauty Parlor	9th Pass	6 Months
27	Typing	9th Pass	6 Months
28	Four Wheeler Driving	8th Pass	35 Days
29	Spoken English Classes	8th Pass	3 Months
30	Gents Parlor (Basic and Advanced Courses)	9th Pass	6 Months
31	Four Wheeler Repairing	9th Pass	6 Months

Source: Field Study and Pamphlet received during personal visit.

8.5.2 Rural Self-Employment Training Institute:

The various areas in which self-employment training is imparted by Rural Self-Employment Training Institute is detailed below:

Rural Self Employment Training Institutes

List of Training Programs

S.No.	Program Area	Type of Program
1	Agricultural Programmes	1. Agriculture and allied activities 2. Dairy Farming 3. Poultry Farming 4. Apiculture 5. Horticulture 6. Sericulture 7. Mushroom cultivation 8. Floriculture 9. Fisheries, etc.

S.No.	Program Area	Type of Program
2	Product Programme	1. Dress designing 2. Rexene articles 3. Incense sticks manufacturing, 4. Football making, 5. Bag making 6. Bakery products 7. Leaf cup making 8. Recycled paper manufacturing, etc.
3	Process Programmes	1. Two wheeler repairs 2. Radio/TV repairs 3. Motor rewinding, electrical transformer repairs 4. Irrigation pump-set repairs 5. Tractor and power tiller repairs 6. Cell phone repairs 7. Beautician course 8. Photography and videography 9. Screen printing 10. Domestic electrical appliances repair 11. Computer hardware and DTP.
4	General Programmes	Skill development for women
5	Other Programmes	Programs related to other sectors like leather, construction, hospitality etc.

Source: http://nirdpr.org.in/rseti/aboutus.aspx

8.5.3 Entrepreneurial Development Training Programme:

The following activities are conducted under the ESDP Scheme

Entrepreneurship Skills Development Programme

S. No.	Program	Duration
1	Industrial Motivational Campaign (IMC)	2 Days
2	Entrepreneurship Awareness Programme (EAP)	2 Weeks
3	Entrepreneurship-cum-Skill Development Programme (E-SDP)	6 Weeks
4	Management Development Programme (MDP)	1 Week

Source: https://msmedi.dcmsme.gov.in/

8.5.4 Women and Children Welfare Scheme:

Following training will be provided under the women and child welfare development scheme to upskill rural women for self-employment and entrepreneurship.

Women and Children Welfare Scheme

S. No.	Program	Description
1	Vocational Training for Women	1. Provided by Pune Municipal Corporation to girls and women. 2. Age Group is 15 to 45 Years. 3. Free bus service is provided for transportation. 4. Fees of Rs. 500/- is taken as deposit which is refundable after course completion. 5. Tool Kit is also provided to the students.

S. No.	Program	Description
2	Self-Employment	1. Pune Municipal Corporation will provide a grant to the rural women of Rs. 5000/- 2. The age group is 18 to 45 years of age. 3. Self Help Group Members will be given preference. 4. Backward Class Women will receive Rs. 10,000/- as a grant.
3	Entrepreneurship Development Program for Women	1. Training on developing skills for Self-Employment will be provided. 2. Age group of the women should be from 18 to 45 years of age.

Source: https://www.pmc.gov.in/en/women-and-child-welfare-scheme

Summary:

The need and importance of training is discussed in this chapter. The chapter describes what value training adds to an individual and how does it make a lot of difference when an individual or rural woman in this case undergo a proper training. The identification of training needs is discussed followed by the areas in which practical training needs to be taken. There are various training institutes which a rural woman can explore in order to avail practical training. Some of the institutes which the author has personally visited and explored through secondary research are mentioned in the chapter. Thus it is concluded that training can be of various types and of various duration as provided by various institutes but the crux is that it should be able to develop the skills of the rural woman so that she can become an entrepreneur and run her own start-up venture.

******

Chapter 9
How to Raise Funds?

उद्यमेन हि सिध्यन्ति, कार्याणि न मनोरथैः ।
न हि सुप्तस्य सिंहस्य प्रविशन्ति मुखे मृगः ॥

In order to get anything a lot of hard work and efforts are required and not just by thinking or imagining about it. It is in the same as a lion cannot get a deer in his mouth just by sleeping he will have to hunt for it.

Learning Objectives:
- To understand the importance of funds.
- To analyze the requirement of funds for running Start-Up.
- To explore the areas where funds are required.
- To discuss on the sources from where funds can be raised.

Learning Outcomes:
- To discuss about the importance of funds
- To describe the requirement of funds for running a Start-Up.
- To explain about the areas where funds will be required.
- To evaluate various sources for raising funds.

Chapter Outline:
9. How to Raise Funds?

9.1 Introduction

9.2 Identification of Funds Requirements

9.3 Areas where Funds will be required

9.4 Sources to Raise Funds

Summary

9.1 Introduction:

Money, money, money, brighter than sunshine and sweeter than honey. Money is not God but neither less than God. For anything and everything money is required. In management we often talk about 7 Ms of Management.

M - Money – deals with "Financial Management".

M - Man – deals with "Human Resources Management".

M - Material – deals with "Materials Management and Inventory Management."

M - Machine – deals with "Production Management'

M - Methods – deals with "Operations Management"

M - Minutes – deals with "Time Management"

M - Management – deals with "Management of all above components".

The First 'M' of the Seven Ms mentioned above is Money. You need money, funds or capital to start a new venture. You may have wonderful ideas, but all the ideas may fail if you don't have money, capital or funds. Hence the First "M" is money. This deals with "Financial Management". If you have money, you can employ 'Men' the human resource. "Man" here means quality human resources.

Every organization whether big or small is run by quality human resource. You may have a very plush infrastructure with all the modern amenities, but if the people working in the organization are not positive in their attitude, then the organization will not grow.

The next 'M' deals with Materials i.e. materials which can be either raw materials which are inputs for a manufacturing unit or it can be materials as finished which can be raw material for other industry. The finished goods of one industry may work as raw material for other industry. Here we also have a component of stock or inventory. We also have the inventory management and the various ways of inventory management in terms of LIFO, FIFO and HIFO methods. The we have another "M" for Machines which deals with Production Management. For production to take place we need to have the right type of machines and equipments as assets or we can say capital. Only having machines is not sufficient. We also need to have proper operations. Thus the next 'M' deals with Operations Management where we deal with Project Evaluation and Review Technique (PERT) and Critical Path Method (CPM).

Finally, time also plays a crucial role hence the next 'M' which talks about minutes deals with Time Management. The order which is taken from the customers has to be processed properly and delivered on time to the customers. Hence time management is crucial and has vital importance. The final 'M' is Management which basically deals with managing all the above mentioned components efficiently and effectively.

When all the Ms are managed efficiently and effectively it will also result is generation of "Money" in terms of Sales and Revenue. Thus the end result of all this is again Money. It is understood that "Money" is required to generate "Money". The ultimate objective of any business whether big or small is Profit Maximization and Cost Minimization which can come through optimization. Thus it can be concluded that all the "Ms" deal with one or the other functional area or specialization area of Management.

9.2 Identification of Funds Requirement:

There are four factors of production – Land, Labour, Capital and Entrepreneur or Enterprise. Against 'Land' we pay 'Rent', against 'Labour' we pay 'Salary' or 'Wages', against 'Capital' we get 'Interest' and "the Entrepreneur" gets "the Profit" for bearing the risk. "Business" is often defined as the capability to bear risk. Higher the risks higher the returns, lower the risk lower the returns. Thus in order to set up any 'Start-Up' or 'Enterprise' in the long run all these factors are important. But the first and foremost important factor is Capital. 'Capital' does not only mean 'money' but has a bigger connotation. "Capital" means all the things which are required to start your business. Beyond money it also means assets (fixed assets) in terms of premises, fans, tube lights, machinery, water, raw materials etc. and the basic things required to start with. For example: If a rural woman wants to start her own tailoring shop or boutique. Then she can start the business from her home as well. Then in that case she won't have to rent a premises to start her own venture. If she already has a sewing machine, then she can use the same and use her own asset to start her venture. The only thing which she will require is money to buy raw materials to start tailoring business. But we cannot limit the requirement here, because funds or money is also required to run the day to day operations. Thus we will require the Fixed Capital as well as the Working Capital.

Thus it becomes imperative to identify how much fund is required to start and set up the Start-Up. Any Start-Up whether big or small will require both Fixed Capital as well as Working Capital. Once the entrepreneur is able to identify how much funds will be required to start the new venture, efforts can accordingly be put to raise the funds.

9.3 Areas where Funds will be required:

There are various areas where funds will be required. Initially when starting a venture, a very well planned Business Plan is a must as it will exhume the areas where money or funding will be required. The amount of capital required for starting a venture will depend on lot many factors. These factors are discussed below.

9.3.1 Type of Venture:

First and foremost, the entrepreneur should be ready with the answers of all the WH Questions.

Why? – Why am I starting this venture? – Need or Requirement

What? – What kind of Start-Up venture am I starting? – Sole Proprietorship, Partnership, Company – Public Ltd. or Private Ltd.

Which? – Which Industry am I going to go for? Whether it will a product or a service? – Decision on Industry, Product or Service.

Where? – Where am I going to set up the Start-Up? (Market) Where from am I going to get the money? (Funding/Finance)

When? – When am I going to Start the Operations of the Start-Up?

Who? – Who are the Customers or Consumers of the Product or Service?

Who are the Suppliers?

Who are the Competitors in the market?

How? – What steps am I going to take to turn a dream into reality?

How will I set up the Start-Up and start its operations?

It is very important to do a thorough home work on the above points, so that the entrepreneur has a clear picture in his or her mind about the startup he or she is willing to set up.

9.3.2 Product or Service: At the outset it is very important to decide and pen down whether the Start-Up will be of products or of Services, or a combination of products or services. For Example: If a rural woman starts a Tiffin Center, then in this case it will be a combination of Product as well as Service. What kind of Tiffin will be provided? What all food will be provided? For how many times the food will be provided? For how many days the food will be provided? Will it be vegetarian food or non-vegetarian food? What will be the mode of payment? Whether we will go for advance payment or daily payment or monthly payment, or will there be coupon system. Who will deliver the tiffins? How the tiffin will be delivered? Are we going to provide Tiffin Services to only households or to the offices, schools, colleges etc.? All these things need to be decided and planned well in advance.

9.3.3 Price of the Product or Service: The price of the product or service has to be kept as per the market condition. We need to understand what kind of market structure is it? Is it a market of Perfect Competition or Imperfect Competition? If Imperfect Competition, then whether it is a Monopoly Market or Monopolistic Market or Oligopoly Market. The price of the product or service will be determined accordingly.

9.3.4 Promotion: The promotional activity will also incur cost. What kind of promotional activity is required will be based on the target market, their educational level and level of acumen and also the tool which will have the maximum reach. For Example: In villages we can reach the village population through SHGs, Radio, mobile phone, Sarpanch or Village Pradhan or by organizing various awareness campaigns at village level or Panchayat Level.

9.3.5 Place/Distribution Channel: The channel of distribution also incurs a cost. What kind of channel of distribution will be used by the women entrepreneur to reach the target customers will determine the cost incurred? Two things can happen. Either the well will go to the person who is thirsty or the thirsty person will come to the well to quench his or her thirst. Hence the decision on distribution channel, whether it will be zero Level, One Level, Two Level or Three Level Channel of Distribution will determine the Cost accordingly. Because every intermediary will be taking his or her share accordingly for making the product or service available from the point of production to the point of consumption.

9.3.6 People: The quality of work force also requires funds. If you want to employ good quality work force to work for you, then you need to pay a good amount of money as salary. The quality of work force matters a lot. The work force may be skilled, semi-skilled or unskilled. All the types whether skilled, semi-skilled or unskilled workers are required at different levels for different kind of work. Along with skill, experience in the field is also of immense importance as if the work force is inexperienced again you need to train them. Hence hiring quality work force is again a cost. You will have to be a good pay master to get quality people at work.

9.3.7 Process: The business model on which your entire Start-Up will work is of immense importance as it will tell you the entire process on which the business will work. Hence the entire process of the business model needs to be thoroughly tested and worked so as to avoid ambiguity and any kind of loss. Incorporation of a proper process or business model also incurs cost.

9.3.8 Market: Offering the product or service in the market will also incur cost. This again depends on the kind of product or the service. The entrepreneur may either have to purchase or take a place or shop on rent to display his or her products or provide the services. In case of digital platform also there is a cost as if you want to create your own website and sell across then you will have to pay for the domain charges and hosting charges. The entrepreneurs can also sell online like through amazon etc. but here to you need to register as a seller and complete the procedure.

9.3.9 Customers: The customers should be properly informed and reached so that the sales can happen and revenue can be generated. Either the seller has to go to the buyer or the buyer has to come to the seller. In both the cases we need to formulate a strategy so that there is foot fall and customers are able to make purchases. Tapping customers also require cost as you need data base to reach out to the customers. For buying data base again there is a cost. For installing a software again there is a cost involved.

9.3.10 Proximity to the Market: The proximity of the seller to the market is again very important. If the seller is in the market itself, then the cost will be minimized, or else procuring the raw material also incurs a cost. The same will be applicable to procure the finished goods. Hence the distance of the market from the seller's house is also a concern as it will also incur some cost.

9.3.11 Area of Operation: The area of operation will also play a significant role as far as the business is concerned. If the entrepreneur is limiting himself or herself to a particular area or region, then the scene will be different. But if the entrepreneur is doing business nationally or internationally through import and export, the complete scenario will be different and will incur a huge amount of cost. The cost again depends on the transaction. In export or import the goods can be bought or sold on credit as well.

9.3.12 Suppliers: Reaching out to the suppliers and getting the raw materials from suppliers will incur a cost. The raw materials will have to be purchased from the suppliers on credit and the payments can be made later on as and when sales take place or based on the payment terms and conditions as negotiated by the suppliers.

9.3.13 Competitors: In order to remain in the market, we need to keep an eye on the competitors. We need to analyze the strategy the competitors are using to remain in the market and generate sales and revenue. Every move of the competitor creates an impact on the sales and hence the entrepreneur need to be vigilant about the same. We need to compete with the competitors in order to gain market share. This also incurs cost as we need to strategize to bring in more customers and retain the existing one.

9.3.14 Transportation: The entire transportation cost has to be worked out including the frequency of the transportation cost. The entire cost required in procuring the raw materials from the point of production to the point of manufacturing or processing needs to be calculated. Beyond this the cost involved in delivering the finished goods from the point of manufacturing or processing to the point of consumption or end consumer needs to be worked out and calculated.

9.3.15 Intermediaries: The intermediaries play a significant role in providing the goods or services to the end user or consumer. Who will be intermediaries, how the product will reach the ultimate consumer for consumption needs to be decided and thoroughly worked out. It is also important to discuss the same with people who are already in this field, to have an insight and know how about the process.

9.4 Sources to Raise Funds:

For any entrepreneur to start a Start-Up, funds are the first and the foremost thing which is required. You can have wonderful ideas, but ideas are like water bubbles which get punctured in absence of suitable funding. To convert a dream into reality funds are required. There are various sources from where the funds can be raised. Here, the focus is on how the Rural Women can raise funds if she is willing to start her own Start-Up. The points mentioned below explain the various sources which a rural woman can explore or use to start her own enterprise of Start-Up.

9.4.1 Own Financial Sources / Personal Savings / Personal Assets: It is often said that money saved is money earned. Rural women can use their personal savings to initially fund their start-up or new venture. Whatever savings she has made can be utilized initially to buy raw materials etc. at the outset for starting up her venture. Later on arrangements can be made to get the funds from various other sources.

9.4.2 Financial Support from Spouse/Husband: The research revealed that the husbands are the supporters of rural women to become entrepreneurs and help them in starting their own venture. This further reveals that the husbands also provide financial support as required by rural woman to plunge into entrepreneurship. The husbands can also use their savings and earnings in setting the start-up venture. Thus rural women get financial support from their husbands as well for starting the venture.

9.4.3 Financial Support from Parents-in-Law: The research further reveals if further required the parents-in-law also can sponsor the venture by providing required money and financial support. This is because the entire family will be benefitted if the venture is created as this will lead to the upliftment of the lifestyle of the family but also provide financial stability.

9.4.4 Financial Support from Parents: The majority of parents of rural women belong to business family and only a few belong to service class. Thus the parents of the rural women can also provide financial support to their daughters if she wants to start her own venture. The entrepreneurial mindset has come from the parents only as the rural women have seen their fathers doing business. Thus rural women can also take financial help and support from parents.

9.4.5 Financial Support from Siblings(Brother/Sister): The research reveals

that rural women come from families where in there are siblings. Thus their siblings can also support them in case of fund requirement. Thus siblings are also sources of funds for starting start-up. Once the firm starts generating revenue and profits the money can be returned to the siblings and parents and all those who have supported her during fund requirement.

9.4.6 Financial Support from Friends or Relatives: If at all required, friends and relatives can also come forward to support in the creation of start-up venture. Thus rural women can also take financial support from friends and relatives. It may happen that rural women will have to convince the relatives and friends and share the start-up venture project and business plan with them as they are going to invest their money in the self-employment start-up venture. Once the relatives and friends are assured that the money is in safe hands and they will get their money back with some returns, they can also provide funds and financial support for entrepreneurship.

9.4.7 Financial Support through Self-Help Groups (Bachat Gats): After visiting various banks it was found that various banks have their special SHG branches who are exclusively involved in providing loans to rural women and rural women entrepreneurs who have registered themselves into some or the other Self Help Group also called as Mahila Bachat Gat. Banks provide loans to rural women and rural women entrepreneurs through Self Help Groups. In order to avail loans rural women will have to become members of SHGs. Banks are financing to SHGs only and not to individual women. They need to do registration in PCMC and bring CA Audit Certificate.

9.4.8 Financial Support from Banks/Money Lenders: Banks take a lot of time to disburse the loans and may require collateral security to give loan. Banks will provide loan to rural women if they are financially sound. Rural women have varied experiences. The perception of rural women in this case is equally positive and negative. Rural women have agreed that banks will ask for immediate repayment of loans. Rural women are capable of repaying the loan taken from banks and financial institutions.

9.4.9 Financial Support Financial Institutions: Financial institutions are not biased in giving loans to rural women. Rural women are eligible to take loans from any financial institution. Rural Women's experience with financial institution speaks that financial institutions take a lot of time for the documentation of loan proposal. They have experienced that getting loan sanctioned from financial institution is very time taking and delaying.

9.4.10 Financial Support through Government Schemes: Rural women are aware about business practices i.e. production, distribution, promotion and selling of the product. Results state that rural women are unaware about government support i.e. various schemes run by government related to women entrepreneurship. The government officials at DIC (District Industries Centre) help in the registration of the MSME (Micro, Small and Medium Enterprises). They also help rural women and youth in establishing their own Micro, Small and Medium Enterprises. MCED (Maharashtra Centre for Entrepreneurship Development) officials also play a very crucial role in entrepreneurship development. It was found that, they are involved not only in planning but they also provide quality training through various training programs in rural pockets. They also monitor the impact of training programmes on rural women in becoming an entrepreneur. They encourage rural women and youth as well in the areas of Entrepreneurship and support them for sustainable development. Beyond this rural woman can also get financial support from government schemes like Annapurna Scheme, Bharatiya Mahila Bank Business Loan, Mudra Yojana Scheme, Orient Mahila Vikas Yojana Scheme, Dena Shakti Scheme, Pradhan Mantri Rozgar Yojana, Udyogini Scheme, Cent Kalyani Scheme, Mahila Udyam Nidh Scheme.

9.4.11 Financial Support through Non-Government Organizations: They are also unaware about the support and help extended by NGOs and SHGs. Rural women are unaware about the support extended by social workers to them but are aware about the channels of distribution to sell their products. Garmin Mahila Va Bal Vikas Mandal an NGO of Bank of Maharashtra supports in formation of the Self Help Groups. This supports rural women in saving and using their own money and getting rid of local money lenders.

GMVBVM supports a lot by forming SHG, providing health facilities to SHG members, providing training and skill development programme. GMVBVM also supports SHG members with the mediclaim and insurance policies, supports rural women in counselling and supporting legally to solve various problems between the family members. GMVBVM also provides marketing services for sale of items and products made by the SHG members, women entrepreneurs and rural artisans.

Bharatiya Yuva Shakti Trust (BYST), a sister concern of CII works on the principle of "Turning Job Seekers into Job Creators". It has tie-ups with several banks and supports in the formation of SHGs through Animators and Coordinators. BYST supports rural youth and women to convert an idea into a feasible business venture. It helps in the entire process starting with the of incubation of the idea to the establishment of the business unit. The units established by rural women or youth are monitored regularly by BYST through Mobile Mentor Clinic. Chapter meetings are conducted every month where mentors and entrepreneurs meet and a culture for Entrepreneurship is developed.

Summary:

This chapter details the importance of fund requirement for starting a venture. It is understood that "Money" is required to generate "Money". The ultimate objective of any business whether big or small is Profit Maximization and Cost Minimization which can come through optimization. In order to set up any 'Start-Up' or 'Enterprise' in the long run all these factors are important. But the first and foremost important factor is Capital. 'Capital' does not only mean 'money' but has a bigger connotation. "Capital" means all the things which are required to start your business. Beyond money it also means assets (fixed assets) in terms of premises, fans, tube lights, machinery, water, raw materials etc. and the basic things required to start with. Thus it becomes imperative to identify how much fund is required to start and set up the Start-Up. Any Start-Up whether big or small will require both Fixed Capital as well as Working Capital. Once the entrepreneur is able to identify how much funds will be required to start the new venture, efforts can accordingly be put to raise the funds.

The various areas where the funds will be required is discussed at length like type of venture, product or service, price of the product or service, promotion and distribution channel, people, process, market, customers, proximity of the market, area of operation, suppliers, competitors, transportation and intermediaries. The chapter further discusses the various sources from where rural women can raise funds. The various government schemes are also mentioned which can be availed to take benefits in order to start the venture of her own by rural women who are looking forward for entrepreneurship.

****

CHAPTER 10
Establishing your Own Start-Up

अश्वस्य भूषणं वेगो मत्तं स्याद् गजभूषणं ।
चातुर्यम् भूषणं नाया- उद्योगो नरभूषणं ॥

A horse is adorned for its speed and an elephant is glorified because of its majestic walk. Similarly, women are appreciated and adorned for their skills and men who are industrious and always engaged in work are appreciated.

Learning Objectives:

- To understand what is a Start-Up?
- Determine the need and importance of Start-Up.
- To develop the ability to establish one's own Start-Up
- To understand the Step by Step Procedure to establish Start-Up.

Learning Outcome:

- To describe what a Start-Up is all about.
- To discuss the need and importance of Start-Up.

- To demonstrate how to establish one's own Start-Up.
- To describe the step by step process involved in establishing Start-Up.

Chapter Outline:
10. Establishing your Own Start-Up:

10.1 Introduction

10.2 What is a Start-Up?

10.3 Need and Importance of Start-Up

10.4 Step by Step Procedure to Establish One's Own Start-Up.

Summary

10.1 Introduction:

Establishment of one's own start-up is the final stage of the entire entrepreneurial process. This is the dream come true for any entrepreneur and especially rural woman in this case as this book deals with 'rural women – the untapped potential'. It is already discussed at the very outset that in order to go for entrepreneurship, the first and the foremost thing is self-analysis which helps us to understand what am I meant for. Once this is clear, then comes the skill analysis which makes us aware what are the skills I have and how can I use those skills. The next very important decision which one needs to take is whether he or she wants to go for Employment and take up a job or will undergo self-employment and entrepreneurship. Only thinking for Self-Employment is not sufficient, you need to have an entrepreneurial mindset. This is utmost important because all of us don't have an entrepreneurial mindset to think on those lines.

Now once it is found that you have an entrepreneurial mindset, it becomes imperative to decide what are the Self-Employment avenues which can be used and are feasible as per the skills required to take up that avenue. It is also understood that once it is decided to take up self-employment we need a proper entrepreneurial environment to convert that dream into a reality. The entrepreneurial environment will help the budding entrepreneur in giving a proper shape to the venture. He or she may also need hand holding so that they can proceed in the right direction and take guidance from expert people in that business. Expert guidance will help in getting rid of several doubts or myths which we may have in mind while planning for the entrepreneurial venture.

Just hand holding is not sufficient as the person who is going to start the venture needs to be adequately trained so that he or she can run the venture smoothly. Hence training organizations play a significant role to upskill and develop the skills. Proper training programs will provide a practical exposure through experiential learning as the budding entrepreneur will learn by doing which is very practical. Training will bring ample amount of confidence in the individual and also develop the required knowledge to be used for the self-employment venture. This will also help in networking with others who have the similar mindset and are looking forward towards self-employment creation. Once the training is done the next thing which comes in the picture is the financial aspect as to how to raise funds. There are various ways through which funds can be raised. The various sources which rural women can use are already discussed at length in the previous chapters.

Now we are at the final stage where everything is already done and now we are at the stage of giving a legal status to the venture. To give a legal status to the venture and finally start its operations requires lots to documentation and legal process which is discussed in this chapter.

10.2 What is a Start-Up?

A Start-Up is a newly formed self-employment venture created by an individual based on his or her entrepreneurial mindset through innovation and creativity which not only creates self-employment but also open doors for employment to others.

Start-Up venture can also be created my more number of likeminded individuals who think in the same direction and want to do something of their own. Start-Up involves lot of creativity and innovation. This leads to the creation of new products or services. Or delivering the products and services in a completely new way etc.

10.3 Need and Importance of Start-Up:

For the upliftment of the society and especially rural areas the creation of start-ups is of immense importance. The rural youth come to urban areas for seeking employment and are not able to cope up with the cut throat competition in the urban areas. They are compelled to go back to villages which leads to frustration. This has its own repercussion in the family and leads to domestic violence and the women in the family has to face the consequences. Start-Up creation will not only make the women a bread earner of the family but also make her self-reliant. She will no more be considered as a burden to the family.

10.3.1 Creates Employment: Start-Up creation by rural women will open lots of employment avenues for rural women living in villages. Thus this decision will not only make rural women self-sustainable but also generate employment for so many other women. Thus they all will be capable of earning their own livelihood. This will also uplift the standard of living of the rural women and their family as well.

10.3.2 Brings Innovation: Creation of start-up will bring innovation. Rural women will be able to create new products and services through their entrepreneurial mindset. Thus people in rural areas will get employment in villages itself and will not think of going outside the village or to cities. Innovation can be of various types. It can be a product innovation or a service innovation. It can also be an innovative way to provide the existing product and service to the existing customers in the market.

10.3.3 New Products and Services: Rural women entrepreneurship and self-employment start-up will create lots of innovative products and services. These innovative products can also be made available in urban areas where people can buy paying a premium price. Thus good quality pure products can be made available to people residing to urban areas.

10.3.4 Revenue Generation: Start-Up creation will lead to revenue and profit generation. Products made by rural women can be bought and sold in urban markets and the money can be given to the rural women. The rural women ventures can be linked in with the urban wholesalers and retailers so that the products can be made available not only in the rural areas but also in the urban areas. Selling products in urban areas can lead to more money as the people living in urban areas will have a high paying capacity as these are the people who are buying from malls.

10.3.5 Village & Society Development: Self-employment through Start-Up venture will lead to development of society and village as well. When rural women will become 'Atma Nirbhar" self-reliant and will start earning her own livelihood through self-employment, so will no more be considered as a burden to the family. Because she is earning not only for herself but for the entire family through her venture. This will change the mindset of the people and women or a girl child will no more be considered a burden to the family. The perception and mindset of people in the society will change. Women will be given equal opportunities to grow and prosper. She will be given proper education and training to stand on her own foot. Thus this will lead to the development of village and ultimately lead to the societal development. Because if you teach a man you are teaching an individual but if you teach a woman you are teaching an entire generation. Society development will further lead to the development of the country.

10.3.6 Urban and Rural Connect: The products made by rural women can be made available in the shopping malls for the urban customers. This will lead to the infrastructural development in terms of construction of roads, electricity and other amenities which will lead to establishment of connection between rural and urban areas. Once this connection is set up, it will also act as a platform to directly reach the rural women entrepreneurs and purchase products from them. Thus, this will lead to the infrastructural development of the villages and the quality of life in villages will also improve.

10.4 Step by Step Procedure to Establish One's Own Start-Up:

To establish a start-up a step by step approach needs to be followed. This will result in giving a legal status or entity to the Start-Up Venture and make it functional. The details of the same is mentioned below:

10.4.1 Naming the Start-Up:

The first and the foremost step is to give a name to the Start-Up. Giving a name to the startup is not an easy task. Lot of things needs to be considered and should be kept in mind when we are going to do this. **The name of the start-up should align or resonate the kind of business we are going to do.** For Example: If rural woman is planning for a Vada Pav business or doing a business of Pakoda. Then the name should be for example Susheela Vada Pav Center or Chetan Pakoda if she wants to keep the name of the venture with her son's name etc. The name itself should reflect the product or the service we are into. **The Keywords should be taken care of while naming the startup**. The keywords should be such that it can easily be remembered. The name of the venture should be such that it is easy to say and understand. We need to **understand he psychology behind keeping this name.** Sometimes we keep the names on Gods or Goddesses because we feel that by their blessings we are able to start this venture. Hence the psychology needs to be understood. We should prevent ourselves from keeping long names of the venture. **The name of the start-up should be short and simple.** The names should not be complicated for people to understand and remember.

10.4.2 Designing the Logo of the Start-Up:

For designing the Logo of the Start-Up professional assistance should be taken from a proper advertising agency. While designing the logo for the Start-Up various parameters like color palette, graphics, font size etc. needs to be taken into consideration so that it makes a direct impact on people and can attract customers. You must explore all the options before picking a suitable choice for your start-up venture.

10.4.3. Legal Formalities:

The various legal formalities required to provide a legal entity to the start-up and bring it to existence requires company registration or registration of the business, tax registration like GST registration, Import Export Code (IEC) if we are planning for export import trade, professional tax registration, Employee State Insurance Registration, Provident Fund Registration and MSME Registration (Udyog Aadhar) etc. which depends on the type of the start-up venture.

10.4.3.1 Company Registration:

At the very out set the self-employment venture or the Start-Up which the rural woman entrepreneur has started needs to be registered under Companies Act 2013. Hence registration of the business is a must. It is again important to understand whether it is a Sole Proprietorship Firm or a Partnership Firm.

10.4.3.1.1 Sole Proprietorship Firm: If it is a Sole Proprietorship Firm, then the registration has to be done at the local authority. It can be town municipality or village gram panchayat in case of a village. **Sole Proprietorship registration is best for Small Businesses.** Rural women should go for this kind of registration. The registration can be done by paying a minimum fee of Rs. 1000/-. Sole Proprietorship registration is best where there are usually less than 5-10 employees. The registration time is 2 to 3 days.

10.4.3.1.2 Separate Legal Entities: When the entrepreneur wants to work separately then he or she can go for **One Person Company**. In this case the entrepreneur is not personally liable if something happens to the company. The registration cost here is somewhere around Rs. 6000/-. The registration time is 5 to 10 days. You are the director and the shareholder of the company. For example, if the name of the Start-Up venture is 'Amir Pakodewala' then after the registration the name will become 'Amir Pakodewala Pvt. Ltd. (OPC)

10.4.3.1.3 Private Limited Company (Pvt. Ltd.): A minimum 2 shareholders and 2 Directors are required for a Private Limited Company. The maximum limit of shareholders for a Private Limited Company is 200 and if you want to make it more than that then you will have to make it a Public Limited Company. In case of a Private Limited Company, there is Limited Liability, so the shareholders here have limited liability. Unfortunately, if something happens to the company, the shareholders are not liable to pay for the losses made by the company. For a Private Limited Company, seed funding becomes easy, as the investors who are investing in the company are also aware about the legal existence of the company. The registration cost is Rs. 7000/-. The time duration required to get the company registered is about 5 to 10 days.

10.4.3.1.4 Limited Liability Partnership: Limited Liability Partnership is mostly for professionals like Doctors, Engineers, Chartered Accountants and architects. Sometimes there are project based partnerships for example in real estate which comes to an end and gets dissolved once the project gets completed.

10.4.3.2 Tax Registrations:

As far as tax registration is concerned, the first and the foremost is the GST registration. If the turnover of your company is more than 20 Lakhs in a year then you have to register for GST. In some of the North States the minimum turnover is 10 Lakhs and GST registration is also required if you deal with import-export trade even within the states or you deal with an e-commerce business.

10.4.3.3 Import Export Code Registration (IEC):

If the start-up venture is into an Import Export business, then you will also need to get the Import Export Code Registration (IEC).

10.4.3.4 Professional Tax Registration:

In some states there are some special types of tax which is called as Professional Tax Registration which you need to get done if you are staying in those states.

10.4.3.5 Employees State Insurance Registration (ESI):

If you have more than 10 employees in your company, then you will have to get Employee State Insurance Registration done.

10.4.3.6 Provident Fund Registration (PF):

If you have more than 20 employees in your start-up venture, then you will have to get even Provident Fund Registration done.

10.4.3.7 MSME Registration (Udyog Aadhar):

MSME Registration or Udyog Aadhar registration is done for Micro Small and Medium Enterprises. The registration will help the venture creator to get many benefits. It will be easier for them to get bank loans. They will also get some tax subsidy, exemption schemes and many such benefits through Udyog Aadhar registration.

10.4.4: Creating the Website:

It is very important to create a website for your start-up. This may act as a challenge for rural women entrepreneurs as they don't have that technical knowhow due to lack of knowledge and education. But if possible they can take help of website developers who can help in creating a website for the rural woman. For creating of the website and webpage it is important to pick up a domain name and a hosting. The domain name is usually named after your brand name to achieve singularity in your brand identity.

After the website is created, it has to be properly designed with all the elements products, services, payment options if any for which support and assistance can be taken from a professional. A professional website designer will help you in providing a proper design as per the need of the Start-Up Venture.

10.4.5: Building the Office:

Building an office for the Start-Up is very important and is even more difficult than creating a website for the Start-Up Venture. Because an office with proper infrastructure, interiors and amenities will provide a professional look to the Start-Up. The entrance should have a proper Board of the Start-Up Venture with the complete name and address. All this may not be possible for a rural woman entrepreneur. If the rural woman us working from home, then she cannot have a separate office. But at least she should have a work place with a proper board of the venture so that people may understand the venture has started and is functional.

10.4.6 Building Work Force or Team:

A rural woman cannot do everything all alone. She needs few people to work with her so that the venture can start working. Thus she can employ few other women who can work with at the venture. This will lead to employment generation and creation of a team. The rural woman entrepreneur should train the other women who have joined her venture so that they can have a good team to take the venture ahead.

10.4.7 Branding, Promotion and Launching the Start-Up:

Brand building is done in order to establish the brand of the start-up. The start-up should have some unique features which will make it different from the others and people and customers will recognize the same and will get attracted. Brand building is a long term activity. When you build a brand identity from the start, it gradually makes its name in the marketplace. Whatever activities do, people notice it and recognize it.

After completing all the above mentioned activities, your startup is now all set for a launch. But before launching and showing your start-up to the world, proper launching campaigns needs to be prepared. It is important to create a hype in the market about the Start-Up Venture launch. If possible then the opening of the venture should be done by a celebrity or in case of Rural woman entrepreneur the Sarpanch can be invited to do the inauguration of the venture followed by an address to the audience.

Some discounts and offers on products should be provided on the opening day so that people will buy the products and register for the services. It should be kept in mind that the date of opening should not clash with any other important date otherwise the footfall of the customers may drop. Press release should be given in the local newspapers and advertisements through pamphlets can be done in the village and nearby villages also.

10.4.8 Growing and Developing the Start-Up:

Once the start-up has started then it is our duty to look forward for its growth and adopt proper strategies accordingly. It is very important to understand the market trends, and keep people informed about the new products available with you. What's App and Facebook can do wonders in providing information. But this may not work in rural areas, because of lack of awareness. In such situations exhibitions can be organized and village fairs can be organized during various festivals where in the villagers go and buy. Door to door visits can also be done to sell the products if required may be in 15 days or once in a month so that the women can buy for themselves and for their family.

10.4.9 Yearly Mandatory Compliances:

There are certain yearly mandatory compliances which needs to be done by every Start-Up owner. These are Filing the Income Tax Return. Every business needs to file Income Tax Return at the end of the year. Every business must do proper Accounting of the Business by maintaining the books of accounts and accounting statements. The GST Return Filing also needs to be done through monthly and quarterly compliances. There is a need to go for Secretarial Compliance if your company is OPC, LLP or Pvt. Ltd. Statutory Audit is also a must if the company is an OPC or LLP and if the company turnover is 40 lakhs or above.

Summary:

The step by step process of establishing a start-up is discussed in detail in this chapter. The chapter describes about what is a start-up and what is the need and importance of setting and starting a Start-Up. The step by step process of approach is discussed starting from naming the venture, designing the logo of the start-up followed by legal formalities.

The legal formalities include registration of the company or the venture, followed by tax registration, ICE Code registration, professional tax registration, employee state insurance registration, provident fund registration and MSME registration (Udyog Aadhar). This is followed by creating a website of the Start-Up venture by purchasing the domain and the hosting. Once the website is created it has to be properly designed by seeking help from professionals. The next step is building a proper office with all the amenities. If it is not possible for rural woman she can use her home and a place at home to run as office and do other operations. The rural woman also needs to develop her own team by employing other rural women from the nearby vicinity. She can train her team as per the requirement of the venture. Now once everything is ready it is the right time for branding, promotion and launch of the venture. Once the venture is launched with proper promotional campaigns, people become aware about the Start-Up. Now the entrepreneur should look forward for the growth of the venture and its sustainability. Certain yearly compliances also need to be taken care of and should be fulfilled.

******

Made in the USA
Monee, IL
08 June 2021